EXPLORING HISTORIC WILTSHIRE
Volume 2: South

Cover: Little Knoll from Long Knoll – see Chapter 8

Alfred's Tower on Kingsettle Hill – see Chapter 9.

EXPLORING HISTORIC WILTSHIRE

Volume 2: South

*Six districts of south Wiltshire:
their history, landscapes and
artistic associations – which
offer the best walking
in the county*

Ken Watts

EX LIBRIS PRESS

Published in 1998 by
EX LIBRIS PRESS
1 The Shambles
Bradford on Avon
Wiltshire   BA15 1JS

Design and typesetting by
Ex Libris Press

Cover printed by
Shires Press, Trowbridge

Printed and bound by
Cromwell Press
Broughton Gifford, Wiltshire

ISBN 0 948578 92 0

This book is dedicated to the late G. B. B.
who loved to walk in Wiltshire.

Contents

About the Author

Ken Watts was born at Devizes in 1933 and has lived for most of his life in Wiltshire. His interest in local history and topography is long-standing, and since his retirement in 1989 from his profession as an architect he has devoted much of his time to these interests. Over the past thirty years he has become familiar with rural Wiltshire by regularly walking in the county and studying its history. For several years he was a Countryside Commission's part-time warden on the Wiltshire section of the Ridgeway, and he has led a great many guided walks in the Wiltshire countryside for many organisations.

In addition to writing this book he took the photographs and drew the maps and line drawings. He has also published *Snap: the History, Depopulation and Destruction of a Wiltshire Village* (1989), *Droving in Wiltshire: the Trade and its Routes* (1990), and *The Marlborough Downs* (1993), as well as magazine articles. He has undertaken detailed research – as yet unpublished – into medieval deer parks and the landscapes of Southern England associated with the life and writings of the poet Edward Thomas.

Author's Note

Throughout this book a number of prehistoric and historical periods are frequently referred to. These periods, with their approximate dates, are as follows:

Neolithic (or New Stone Age): BC 3500 to 2000.
Bronze Age: BC 2000 to 800.
Iron Age: BC 800 to AD 43.
Romano-British: AD 43 to 410.
Post-Roman: AD 410 to 500.
Anglo-Saxon: AD 500 to 1066.
Medieval: 1066 to 1485.
Tudor: 1485 to 1603.
Stuart: 1603 to 1714.
Georgian: 1714 to 1837.
Victorian: 1837 to 1901.

Introduction

This book is written for those who believe that one of the strongest aspects of the countryside is not visual but lies in the invisible history that lies concealed in the landscape. It is the culmination of many years spent by its author walking rural Wiltshire, researching its history, leading guided walks, and acquiring the knowledge which is now passed on to his readers. This is the second of two volumes devoted to exploring on foot the rural parts of Wiltshire. The present volume covers six extensive areas of South Wiltshire south of the Vale of Pewsey. A previous volume *Exploring Historic Wiltshire; Volume 1: North* described six areas north of and including the Pewsey Vale.

The importance of the historical background to landscape was aptly expressed by Hilaire Belloc when he wrote in *The Old Road* (1904): 'By the recovery of the Past, stuff and being are added to us; our lives which, lived in the present only, are a film or surface, take on body – are lifted into one dimension more. The soul is fed', and in *The South Country* (1909) Edward Thomas, a connoisseur of the landscape of the south of England, wrote: 'There are many places that nobody can look upon without being consciously influenced by a sense of their history'.

This book describes the walking that is available in six of the finest districts of rural South Wiltshire. The topography of those areas and the way in which man has moulded the landscape is described, as is the visible prehistory and the history of the areas described and their literary associations, aspects which although not visible add a vital extra dimension to appreciation and enjoyment of the landscape. Although its subjects have been researched in depth, this is essentially an outdoor book intended for those who wish to explore the rural parts of Wiltshire.

From long experience of leading innumerable guided walks over many years I have become aware that many walkers with a feeling for the past wish to know something of the history that lies behind the landscapes in which they walk. As for myself, when walking in an unfamiliar landscape I find myself irritated at my lack of knowledge of its historical background ; that landscape lacks the vital extra dimension which a knowledge of its history would provide. The field antiquities are described as components in the landscape, and the history and literary associations are closely related to the countrysides described. It is written both for local people who wish to extend their walking into new districts, and for those who do not yet know

Wiltshire but are interested in exploring the county.

In *The Making of the English Landscape* (1955) Professor W.G. Hoskins demonstrated that the English landscape is a palimpsest upon which the history of England is visibly etched to be read by the informed observer. He suggests that one cannot understand the English landscape and enjoy it to the full 'without going back to the history that lies behind it'. Professor Hoskins also suggested that poets make the best topographers, and it was the poet Edward Thomas, who loved Wiltshire, who noted in *The South Country* (1909) that 'the landscape retains the most permanent marks of the past'.

This book describes what Professor Hoskins called the 'observables' in the landscape. It is written for those who in their walking in South Wiltshire wish to know of the history that lies concealed behind the visible landscape of Wiltshire, a county which is particularly richly endowed with archaeological field monuments and historical associations. Each chapter takes as its subject a specific area which offers good walking, and provides a wide-ranging in-depth study of the landscape and its associations.

Many walkers recognise that almost as much pleasure is obtained from planning walks as from walking them. Consequently much scope is left for readers to use this book as a basis for devising their own walks to take in those landscape features which interest them – always following the public rights of way shown on the Landranger or Pathfinder Ordnance Survey maps. Nevertheless, for less experienced walkers, each chapter ends with a number of suggestions for walks in general terms. These suggestions are in no way comprehensive; the 'Suggested walks' sections simply describe routes of walks which the author has particularly enjoyed which readers may choose to follow.

Wiltshire is dominated by the Downs. About two-thirds of the county lies on the chalk and everyone who would know Wiltshire must know her Downs. For this reason the greater part of this book is devoted to the areas of chalk downland which are at the very heart of the county. Well known areas are included, as are some less well known landscapes.

A desirable characteristic in any walking book is that it should be compact and portable. This book is consequently reasonably small in format. Some outline maps are included, but it is emphasised that these are merely sketch maps included to indicate the locations of places mentioned in the text. They contain insufficient detail to be regarded as walking maps and are no substitute for the Ordnance Survey maps which, with their definitive indication of all public rights of way are essential for all walkers in England. Two sheets of the 1:50 000 Landrangers maps (numbers 183 and 184) cover most of South Wiltshire, and the numbers of the relevant Landranger maps are given at the head of each chapter. The larger scale Explorer maps are an alternative to the Landrangers.

In order to avoid the necessity for long descriptions of location in rural areas where landmarks are few, six-figure map references are sometimes used in brackets in the text – for example (149763). These references are to the National Grid and refer to the Ordnance Survey maps. The prefixes ST and SU relevant to Wiltshire have been omitted from all map references in the interests of brevity. An explanation of the easily mastered National Grid reference system is given on all Ordnance Survey maps.

It remains to me to make some acknowledgements, first to the staff of Wiltshire Local Studies Library and Wiltshire Record Office for unfailing assistance. Then to my friend Michael Higham with whom I have walked more miles than with any other person over the past thirty years, and to all the people – many of them unknown to me by name on guided walks – with whom I have walked and talked when acquiring the knowledge that has gone into this book. I also acknowledge my indebtedness to the writings of the late Professor W.G. Hoskins and the theories on the evolution of the landscape which he first propounded in *The Making of the English Landscape* (1955):

> The English landscape itself, to those who know how to read it aright, is the richest historical record we possess. There are discoveries to be made in it for which no written documents exist, or have ever existed   There is no part of England, however unpromising it may appear at first sight, that is not full of questions for those who have a sense of the past.

Ken Watts
Trowbridge, Wiltshire,
January 1998.

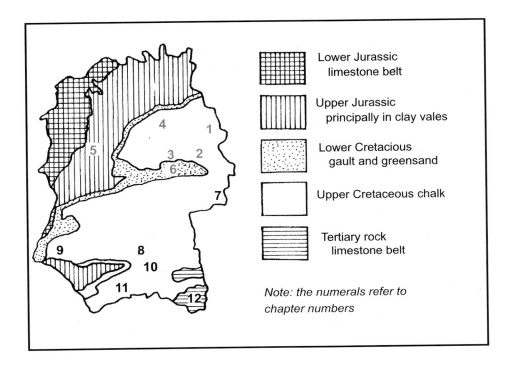

Above: Geological Map of Wiltshire

Opposite: Map of Wiltshire indicating the 12 districts featured in Exploring Historic Wiltshire.
Districts 1-6: Volume 1 North;
Districts 7-12: Volume 2 South.

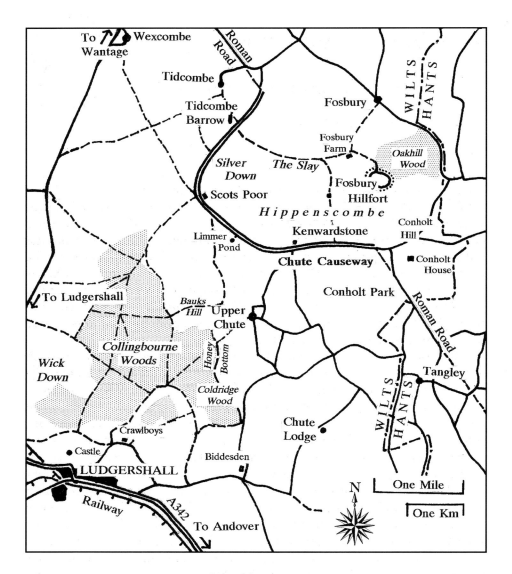

Chute Causeway

7 Chute Causeway

including Collingbourne Woods

(maps Landranger 174 and 184)

Roman Roads

Roman roads are, since they usually provide long standing rights of way across the countryside, always of interest to walkers. An unresolved matter concerning the Roman road system in England is the rapidity and effectiveness with which it was planned and constructed in hostile and unfamiliar countrysides such as Wessex which had strongly opposed the Roman conquest. This remains something of a mystery, particularly when it is remembered that the Romans lacked both adequate maps and the compass. The late G. Bernard Berry spent a lifetime studying this matter and subscribed to a theory that the Roman road system was pre-planned before the Roman Conquest was undertaken.

The first roads to be constructed were the arterial military roads which were built for military purposes in connection with the conquest and the holding down of the new province. These military roads were enhanced by a network of secondary new roads and Romanised native ways which served more local and commercial purposes. Such a Romanised way was the straight track south of the River Wylye (see Chapter 8) sometimes known as the 'Market Way' which served the Roman trading centre of Stockton Earthworks.

A distinctive feature of most Roman roads is their construction in straight alignments. Roman roads were, even where they curved, generally set out in a series of straight sections. This straightness was not simply a matter of convenience, nor that the shortest way between two points is a straight line. It probably arose from the method by which Roman roads were set out.

The Roman practice of using beacons and fires for direction finding – for example in their lighthouses such as the Pharos at Alexandria in Egypt and the lighthouse at Dover which was built soon after the Roman Conquest to guide cross-Channel traffic – is well established, and it seems probable that fires were used to set out their roads. Having identified the points to be

15

joined by the road, which were generally a great distance apart, the alignment could have been maintained over long distances by lighting fires on elevated sighting points at the extremities, and then introducing intermediate mobile fires in cressets which could be adjusted into line, in much the same way that a modern land surveyor lines up his ranging rods. In fact on the Roman road which provides the basis of this chapter Thomas Codrington, the author of *Roman Roads in Britain* (1903) and a civil engineer by profession, recorded finding remains of fires under the metalling of the Roman road in Conholt Park.

Chute Causeway

The usual characteristic of straightness is not an invariable feature of Roman roads. In the extreme east of Wiltshire about four miles north-east of Ludgershall the Roman road from Winchester (the Roman *Venta Belgarum*) to Cirencester (*Corinium*) executes a very unusual four mile long semi-circular deviation from its true line in order to avoid a steep coombe. In the south of England Roman roads frequently ignored natural features, but the Roman surveyor here, as his road left Conholt Park on the Hampshire border, found himself confronted by the steep plunge of over 165 feet (50 m) into Hippenscombe lying across his line. Faced by a natural obstruction of this magnitude the reaction of the Roman road-builder was to accept the inevitability of a diversion from the true line of his road and engineer a long loop around the coombe. This diversion was set out in a series of straight sections past Limmer Pond, Scot's Poor and Tidcombe long barrow, before resuming the true line of the road half a mile south-west of Oxenwood. This long roughly semi-circular diversion is today followed by the modern road and is known as Chute Causeway.

The 'Chute' element of the name – which was also applied to the nearby village of Chute and to Chute Forest as well as to the Causeway – is said by *The Place-Names of Wiltshire* to be derived from the Old British word ceto meaning 'wood' ; the 'causeway' element reflects the fact that the road is raised above the normal ground level, its agger being on average about 27 feet (8.2m) wide with the causeway raised up to 4 feet (1.2m) above the adjoining ground level.

This diversion adopted by the Roman road around Chute Causeway has sometimes been described as unique, but this is not the case. Chute provides the most dramatic example of a diverted Roman road – at least in Wiltshire and probably in England – but near Stratford Tony in south Wiltshire the Roman road from Old Sarum to Badbury Rings follows a similar diversion to avoid the head of a coombe, but on a lesser scale, in a less dramatic situation,

Above: Looking north across Hippenscombe from Kenwardstone which lies in the pit middle right.
Below: Chute Causeway looking west from near Kenwardstone.

and on a length of Roman road that is less positively identifiable on the ground than is Chute Causeway (this example, which also follows its diversion in a series of straight lengths, will be described later, in Chapter 11).

The Romans usually constructed their roads using local materials. In the Wessex chalklands they generally used flints quarried directly from the chalk. The many pits which still exist beside Chute Causeway probably originated as quarry pits excavated to provide materials for the road and its causeway, although when in 1734 this same Roman road was excavated in Conholt Park, a little west of Chute Causeway where its agger is very pronounced, the Roman road was found to be of a layered construction using imported gravel which is alien to this district.

Describing Chute Causeway in *English Downland* (1936), H.J. Massingham wrote:

> If you wind up from Weyhill and Appleshaw to the south, you burst from the umbrageous corridors of Chute Forest up into the high aerial solitude of the rim of the great open bowl. The Roman road, an adaptation of the much older trail, is forced to make a great curve south and east from Scot's Poor to Conholt Park where it recovers the straight, and drops down in a bee-line for Winchester. It always pleases me to catch a Roman road bending... You drift, almost float along the Causeway, while the land falls steeply away on your left into a huge green cauldron, two hundred feet deep, whose downward rushing sides are clothed in gold by the late summer ragwort. This is Hippenscombe. On the opposite side rises Haydown Hill, chequered with the low banks of the Celtic tilth, and with the Celtic citadel of Fosbury, connected by a track with Tidcombe Long Barrow, thrusting out its revetment from the woods behind. Height and depth, distance and neighbourhood feed a sensory delight in them all. It is fitting, therefore, that the great Causeway should offer a something unique in downland.

The Wiltshire-based writer Geoffrey Grigson was similarly impressed by Chute Causeway and memorably described Hippenscombe as lying 'inside a nest of circling contour lines', a phrase which recalls the essayist C.E. Montague who writing of the joy of reading maps in 'When the Map is in Tune' (from *The Right Place: a Book of Pleasures:* 1924) referred to occasions 'when the contour lines begin to sing together', and compared reading a contoured map to reading a musical score.

Apart from providing 'something unique in downland' (Massingham) the area around Chute Causeway offers excellent walking in an area comparatively unfrequented by walkers. As Massingham suggested, it is probably best approached from the extensive broken woodlands of Collingbourne Woods to its south – although he called the woods 'Chute Forest'. From these woods the walker emerges on to the Causeway which runs round a rim of the downs overhanging the great hollow of Hippenscombe, with views of the chequer boarded prehistoric field systems and the great Iron Age fortress of Fosbury on the opposite side of the coombe. The walk along Chute Causeway is a dramatic one. It follows a minor road, but that road is very lightly used by both traffic and walkers, for Chute Causeway is practically unknown as a walking area and I cannot recall seeing another walker other than my own companions walking along the Causeway.

Kenwardstone

Several things of interest may be seen when following Chute Causeway. Interesting stones have featured in many of my earlier descriptions of the Wiltshire countryside, from the standing stones and the sarsen stones of the Marlborough Downs to 18th century milestones beside turnpike roads. Such stones have fascinated innumerable people, for example the artist Paul Nash (1889-1946) who became almost obsessed with the stones of Avebury which he photographed as individuals, and used as the inspiration for his series of paintings called 'Land of the Megaliths' in which the stones were depicted in relation to the landscape. In his *Picture History* Paul Nash left a description of how much such stones meant to him:

The preoccupation of the stones has always been a separate pursuit and interest aside from that of object personages. My interest began with the discovery of the Avebury megaliths when I was staying at Marlborough in the Summer of 1933 they were always wonderful and disquieting... Their colouring and pattern, their patina of golden lichen, all enhanced their strange forms and mystical significance.

Beside Chute Causeway lies a recumbent stone that has attracted a great deal of speculation about its origin. Within one of the pits beside the Causeway which was probably excavated to provide material for the construction of the Roman road, on its north side opposite the junction with the road which runs south to Upper and Lower Chute, lies a large prostrate sarsen stone known as Kenwardstone or Kinwardstone (303552). In 1936 H.J. Massingham drew attention in *English Downland* to the existence of this interesting stone:

> As you begin the long straight bit [of Chute Causeway] going eastwards towards Vernham Dean at the eastern end of the combe you notice an artificial depression a few yards from the Roman road. At the bottom of it lies a prostrate sarsen, some six feet by four and a half. Behind its lichenous encrustation you can detect that it is incised with rippling lines branching out from a kind of tremulous fluted trunk. This is the Kenwardstone and Dr Williams-Freeman aptly compares it with the sculptured stone of Carnac, also megalithic, and, I might add, a Breton descendant of the stone monuments with spiralform carving of Spain, Malta and Crete. The Chute monolith is very possibly the last survivor of a chambered long barrow that lay beside the road from Stonehenge to the Sussex Downs twenty centuries before it was metalled by the Roman engineers.

In his 'Gazetteer of Sites' to *The Archaeology of Wessex* (1958), L.V. Grinsell mentions 'a stone called Kinwardstone south of Savernake' as being at a hundred moot site. There is a Kenwardstone Hundred and *The Place-Names of Wiltshire* (1939) notes 'Cyneweard's Stone' as the site of the meeting place at Kinwardstone Farm, and continues to mention that Kinwardstone Farm was *Kynewardeston* in the 1282 *Inquisitions post mortem*. Kinwardstone Farm is found between Burbage and West Grafton (at 238606) about five miles from the present position of Kenwardstone, and many years ago an old labourer recalled helping to cart the Kenwardstone from a farm to a position beside Chute Causeway. The Rev. G.H. Engleheart recorded in *Wiltshire Archaeological Magazine* (Volume 43) that he had been told in 1897 'the stone had been carted to where it lies from a field on one of the farms where there were many big stones with it'. He concluded that the surface markings on the Kenwardstone were the result of natural weathering.

In *The Folklore of Ancient Wiltshire* (1990) Katherine Jordan wrote:

In an open field a few yards north of the causeway, overlooking Black Down and Hippingscombe, there used to lie a flat stone with strange wavy markings upon it, supposedly known as Kinwardstone (SU 310554 area)... However, it does not seem to be in its place any more.

During the past thirty years I have frequently visited this stone when walking in the area of Chute Causeway. Kathleen Jordan's map reference is incorrect and must explain her having missed it. The stone may still be seen (at 303552), half embedded in the earth and in summer half concealed by the long grass.

Much mystery and folklore becomes attached to such old stones. The top surface of this stone is incised with a series of wavy lines, a fact which led a local shepherd to inform the archaeologist H. St George Gray that the stone was known as the 'Devil's Waistcoat'. Both H.J. Massingham and Dr Williams-Freeman accepted Kenwardstone as a sculpted monolith surviving from a former Neolithic long barrow which had existed long before the Romans constructed their road past it. I hate to pour cold water on an interesting suggestion, but my own opinion is that the marks on Kenwardstone are the result of natural weathering.

Roadside Ponds

It is noticeable when walking in this area that many clumps of old Scots pines are associated with Chute Causeway. This species of tree is known to have been planted to mark droveways, and where mature Scots pines occur in clumps a droveway is to be suspected. It seems likely that Chute Causeway, being an ancient communication route, was used for droving cattle and sheep. This suggestion is supported by the existence on these otherwise arid uplands beside the Causeway of the pine-surrounded Limmer Pond a few yards south of the Causeway (at 293533) and Ashmore Pond (314552), also beside Chute Causeway in the north-west corner of Conholt Park two miles east of Limmer Pond.

Limmer Pond, which was marked 'Pond' by Andrews and Dury on their 1773 map of Wiltshire, is very ancient and was probably used by drovers to water their stock when following the Causeway on their way east into Hampshire. Embedded as it is in thick woodland and surrounded by massive old Scots pines, it retains a particularly venerable feeling despite having recently undergone a tidying-up which could so easily have ruined its atmosphere – and indeed did so for a time – but it has now recovered and has become overgrown once more. Ashmore Pond was *Asshemere* (meaning 'the pond of the ash tree') in 1300 when it was one of the boundary marks of the Hippenscombe Bailiwick of Savernake Forest. The fact that Savernake extended as far as this point in the Middle Ages led to prolongued disputed claims about whether Hippenscombe was in Savernake Forest or Chute Forest.

Fosbury Farm (314570), on the high ground a little north-west from Fosbury hillfort, is an attractive building group in its remote situation. Although the structure is not particularly old it has a venerable feel about it and its situation and atmosphere suggests that a building has long existed here. This may be the site of a former lodge of the Forest of Savernake when that forest was claimed to extend over Hippenscombe, or it could have been an outlying lodge of Chute Forest. In 1773 Andrews and Dury showed Fosbury Farm with the approach to the hillfort running south of it and entering Fosbury on its north-west rather than its present line which passes north of the farm and enters the hillfort on its north side.

Scot's Poor

At the south-western extremity of Chute Causeway, at the point where it swings north to cross Silver Down, is the intriguingly named Scot's Poor (286562), mentioned as an inn by Grundy in *The Ancient Highways and Tracks of Wiltshire*. The derivation of the name is uncertain and *The Place-Names of Wiltshire* begs the question. My own theory is that this place, which appeared as an inn in an 1867 directory, derives its name from 'Scot ales' which were one of the irregular profits made by foresters in royal forests.

'Scot' comes from the Old Norse *skot* meaning a payment. This method of profitmaking was a form of unofficial taxation which presumably explains the often-used expression 'scot-free'. The practice of the foresters was to set up an ale house and extort money from the people living in the forest – who were already subject to a particularly oppressive code of law known as Forest Law – by requiring them to spend their money at their inn, thus further impoverishing them.

Scot's Poor is at the northern extremity of Collingbourne Woods which were formerly the royal Forest of Collingbourne. It was *Staet Geat* in the Great Bedwyn charter of 1213 (probably a mistake for *Straet Geat*, particularly as it was *Street Gate* on an 1825 estate map). In 1773 it was *Scott Poor* on Andrews and Dury, and in the early 20th century an inn, marked by the Ordnance Survey the Blue Bell Inn, still existed at Scot's Poor. The archaeologist O.G.S. Crawford, who became archaeological officer to the Ordnance Survey, visited Scot's Poor in 1914 at about the time that it ceased to function as an inn and believed that he could have been its last customer.

Looking north from Tidcombe long barrow.

Tidcombe Barrow

The beautifully sited Tidcombe Neolithic long barrow (293576), situated one mile north-east of Scot's Poor on Tidcombe Down, has a chamber formed of sarsen stone at its southern end. This barrow, which is about 180 feet (55m) long and about 10 feet (3m) high, was in the distant past badly damaged by villagers who excavated it in 1750 in search of treasure. From Tidcombe Barrow long views may be enjoyed to the west and north, with the reconstructed Wilton windmill prominent three miles to the north-west near Wilton village, past which runs the continuation of the Roman road after it has left Chute Causeway in its progress north-west through Savernake Forest to the Roman town of *Cunetio* at Black Field near Marlborough.

A pronounced prehistoric linear earthwork (286580) runs along Tidcombe Down and passes Tidcombe Barrow before crossing Chute Causeway and continuing east of the way over Round Hill. This earthwork, which is probably part of a Bronze Age enclosure, is best seen from the lane (at about 294574) which runs east from Tidcombe Barrow towards The Slay and Fosbury hillfort.

Restored windmill at Wilton.

Fosbury Hillfort

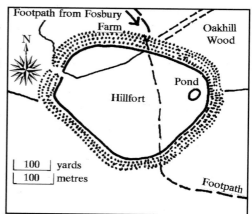

Two miles east of Tidcombe Barrow is Fosbury Hillfort (320564), a double-banked Iron Age hillfort with an entrance to its east. Enclosing an area of 24 acres, Fosbury is one of the largest Wiltshire hillforts. The beech trees growing on its ramparts have had their vast fan-shaped root systems exposed by weathering in a most interesting manner. From Fosbury there are long views east into Hampshire, and shorter ones across Hippenscombe to Chute Causeway which occupies the southern skyline.

Hippenscombe from Conholt Hill with Fosbury hillfort, right.

In Hippenscombe below Chute Causeway, Andrews and Dury show in addition to Hippenscombe Farm under Fosbury a building on 'Black Down' (at 301556) to its west which appeared as 'Blackdown Barn (in ruins)' on the

First series 2.5-inch map. It has now entirely disappeared. Andrews and Dury also show 'Black Down Warren' a little east of Scot's Poor, indicating that rabbit or hare warrening was formerly carried on in this district in the times when winter meat was scarce and rabbits, hares, swans, pigeons and deer, all of which were to some extent farmed, satisfied the need for winter meat.

Collingbourne Woods

The area between Chute Causeway and Ludgershall, three miles to its south-west, is occupied by the extensive woodlands of Collingbourne Woods, formerly the Forest of Collingbourne. Although nearer to Ludgershall than Collingbourne – and Ludgershall was a very important place in early medieval times – these woods take their name from Collingbourne, being in the parish of Collingbourne Kingston. An early medieval deer park was created in these woods in 1253 by William de Valence (died 1296), a French knight and a half-brother to Henry III, who caused resentment by inviting many French knights to the English court at a time when the king of England still had very extensive holdings in France.

By 1275 the parishes of Collingbourne Ducis and Collingbourne Woods were held by the Duchy of Lancaster, which explains the Ducis suffix, although it was still named *Colyngeborn Valence* in 1289. The southern part of Collingbourne Woods had by 1464 been made into a chase known as Collingbourne Ducis Chase and this chase was associated with Crawlboys, the keepership going with the holder of Crawlboys, now Crawlboys Farm (273514). From 1399, when the Duchy of Lancaster estates went to the Crown after the son of John of Gaunt usurped the throne as Henry IV, to the time when it was granted to the Duke of Somerset in the 16th century, Collingbourne was technically a royal hunting forest, and it continues to be designated Collingbourne Forest on modern maps.

William de Valence, who created Collingbourne Park in 1253, was well connected, being a half-brother to Henry III. This suggests that although the royal castle of Ludgershall immediately south of Collingbourne Woods had its own Crown hunting parks from 1203, the early medieval monarchs during their almost continuous 'progresses' around the countryside and their many visits to Ludgershall – which was one of six royal castles – would have hunted over Collingbourne Woods long before these woods became a royal hunting forest.

It is almost certain that the William Collingbourne who was barbarously executed in 1484 for having been in treasonable contact with Henry Tudor at the time when he was challenging Richard III's right to the throne, came from Collingbourne. It is known that in 1441 William Collingbourne was granted Everleigh Park, situated west of Collingbourne, for life. That he was a servant of Richard III's mother Cecily Neville we know from a letter written by King Richard to his mother in which William Collingbourne is mentioned as having been her officer in Wiltshire at the time when Collingbourne was a royal forest. At that time second names were often an indication of the place of birth of the bearer of the name.

Collingbourne was accused of having originated and pinned to the door of St Paul's Cathedral the famous political couplet:

> *The Cat, the Rat, and Lovel our dog,*
> *Rule all England under a hog.*

In this couplet Collingbourne denounced Richard III and three of his closest supporters, 'the Cat' being William Catesby and 'the Rat' Sir Richard Ratcliffe. Lovel was Francis, Lord Lovel who owned properties in Wiltshire at Elcombe (Chapter 3 of Volume 1) and Upton Lovell (Chapter 8). The 'hog' was a reference to Richard III's badge, a wild boar. Whether or not he was the originator of the clever couplet, Collingbourne was tried for it, was found guilty, and was hanged, drawn and quartered as a traitor on Tower Hill in 1484. Men were stoical in those days; when he was hanged but cut down alive and his heart cut out and thrown on the fire he was heard to mutter 'Jesus, Jesus – more trouble'. The following year he was avenged when Henry Tudor invaded, killed Richard III at Bosworth, and usurped the throne.

The terrain of Collingbourne Woods is undulating and the woodland very broken, particularly at its north edge around Bauks Hill (285539) on Chute Down, the great bluff of open downland which cuts into the woodland. On Bauks Hill a series of connected banked and ditched linear earthworks may be prehistoric, although they cross a prehistoric field system, have the appearance of being medieval, and could be the substantial remains of William de Valence's early medieval deer park pale. Anyone walking in Collingbourne Woods should try to visit Bauks Hill which almost disconnects the western part of Collingbourne Woods from their eastern section known as Coldridge Wood, where Andrews and Dury in 1773 show a forest lodge as Collingbourne Lodge' (at 286529). Here on Bauks Hill deer still wander, and many buzzards wheel and cry above this great gap in the extensive woodlands. Mention of these great birds of prey is a reminder that the expanse of downland west of Collingbourne Forest was in the late-16th century celebrated for falconry, as was Collingbourne Forest for the hunting of deer. Henry VIII granted Everleigh to Sir Ralph Sadler who became falconer to Queen Elizabeth and also served as one of the three commissioners entrusted with trying to arrange a tripartite settlement between Queen Elizabeth, Mary Queen of Scots, and the future James I. He became for a time the jailer of the Queen of Scots, and found himself in trouble with Queen Elizabeth for allowing his charge too much freedom and permitting her to join him in his favourite sport of hawking.

The extent of the woodland of Collingbourne Woods today remains very much as shown by Andrews and Dury in 1773, except that the woods to the north-east towards Limmer Pond are now reduced. Wick Down to the south-west of the woods was Old Windmill Hill' on the 1773 map.

Down the east edge of Coldridge Wood runs Honey Bottom, a name which is like Honey Street in the Vale of Pewsey presumably a comment on the glutinous state of the trackway, and at the west edge of Coldridge Wood is Coldridge Bottom which runs south towards Faberstown. Collingbourne Woods is one of the few locations in Wiltshire where beech trees regenerate naturally.

In reflecting on this area four memories spring immediately to mind. First comes the mysterious Kenwardstone which has exercised the minds and imaginations of so many people over so many years, and then there are the recollections of many visits to the beautifully situated hillfort of Fosbury with its long views east into Hampshire. The third recollection is of walking in the fine woodlands of Collingbourne Woods, but the abiding memory is of walking along the Chute Causeway, enjoying the constantly changing views as the way follows its broad arc around the rim of the coombe in the footsteps of the Romans who here, when confronted by the great valley of Hippenscombe, were obliged to depart from their usual practice of constructing their highways across country in straight lines and make the long diversion which we call today Chute Causeway. The great pity is that the Roman causeway has been adopted as a modern road and macadamed. What a walk this would be if it were still a remote Roman way which had been left alone and not adopted by modern traffic. The redeeming feature is the fact that the traffic in this remote upland situation in the extreme east of Wiltshire is comparatively light.

Suggested Walks around Chute Causeway

7A: Chute Causeway to Rivar Down (10.5 miles: map 174):

North from Chute Causeway the walking is inevitably across Hippenscombe from Little Down (312552) where a car may be conveniently left. One walk to the north is to Rivar Down and Rivar Hill. The coombe bottom is crossed at Hippenscombe Farm and the walk continues north across The Slay. At a crossing of tracks (309568) continue north passing Beacon Farm and between Tidcombe and Oxenwood villages and to Botley Down, then north-east along Rivar Down (307610) to Rivar Hill. From Rivar Hill the walk may be extended along the ridgeway over Ham Hill, briefly entering Hampshire a little before the way reaches Inkpen Hill with its gibbet and Walbury Hill, at 974 feet (297m) the highest point in Hampshire. On Ham Hill this ridgeway passes above the former home of the writer Lytton Strachey (1880-1932) at Hamspray House (342631), the house where he died in 1932 and where a few weeks later his friend the artist Dora Carrington committed

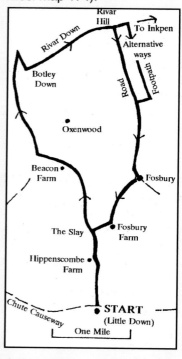

suicide. Our route is south from Rivar Hill (317613) down the minor road or the parallel footpath to its east to Fosbury village. From Fosbury the way back to Little Down is south past Fosbury Farm, across The Slay, and past Hippenscombe Farm back to Little Down on Chute Causeway.

7B: Chute Causeway to Fosbury Hillfort (6 to 8 miles: map 174):

An interesting circular walk of about 6 miles may be taken by parking near the trigonometrical point (312552) on Little Down and following Chute Causeway west past Kenwardstone (303552), Limmer Pond (293553) and Scot's Poor (286562) to Tidcombe long barrow (293576). From here, after turning east, The Slay may be crossed above the north side of Hippenscombe on the approach from the west to Fosbury hillfort past Fosbury Farm. The hillfort provides fine views across Hippenscombe to Chute Causeway and east into Hampshire. A short return towards The Slay brings walkers (at 309568) to a cross track which runs south across the Hippenscombe and climbs its south side back to the start point. This 6 mile walk may be extended by 2 miles by continuing east from Fosbury hillfort, descending the downs along the footpath which follows the south edge of Oakhill Wood towards

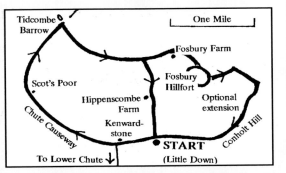

Vernham Dean in Hampshire, and at the road turning south and following the road up Conholt Hill past Conholt Park to the starting point.

7C: Chute Causeway into Collingbourne Woods

(8 miles: maps 174 and 184):

South from Chute Causeway excellent woodland walking is available into Collingbourne Woods. One mixed down and woodland walk commences from a point near New Zealand on Chute Causeway (289557) half way between Scot's Poor and Limmer Pond. The route is south over Mount Cowdown and Bauks Hill with its interesting linear earthworks, west of Coldridge Wood and then southwest past Crawlboys Farm (273514) north of Ludgershall. From Blackmore Down west of Crawlboys the way back to Chute Causeway is north up the west edge of Collingbourne Woods over Wick Down and Sunton Heath through Shaw Cross (276550) and past Gammon's Farm to Scot's Poor.

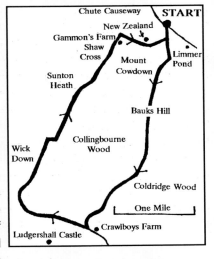

West from Chute Causeway the countryside consists of broad open practically untreed downlands with extensive views to the north. From Scot's Poor and Tidcombe long barrow several paths run west over Fairmile and Wexcombe Downs towards Collingbourne Kingston and Wexcombe village, West and East Grafton, and Wilton village situated beside Wilton Water and the Kennet and Avon Canal. Half a mile east of Wilton is the reconstructed Wilton windmill.

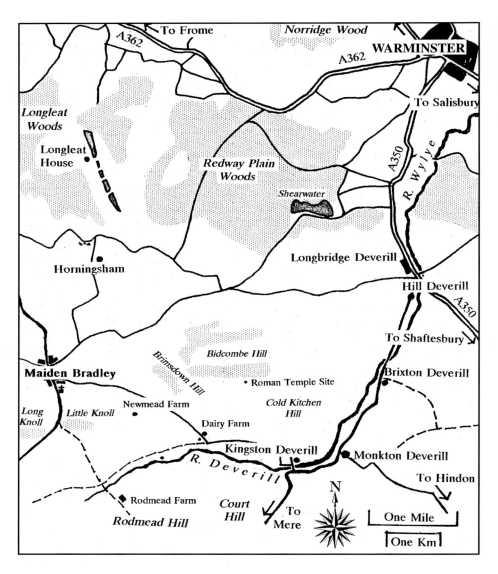

The Deverill Valley (the Upper Wylye)

8   The Wylye Valley

including the Deverill or Upper Wylye

(maps Landranger 183 and 184)

Wiltshire, with its great land masses of chalk downland and its many dry upland coombes, suffers from a lack of good rivers compared with some of its neighbouring counties. The River Wylye and its headwaters, generally known as the Deverill – which gives its name as the second name-place element to a series of fine villages – goes some way to remedying this deficiency.

The Wylye – with two 'y's in such a short name – is an improbable name which has presented difficulties in both spelling and pronunciation to those unfamiliar with the name, and its etymology is admitted to be uncertain. The name originated before the Norman Conquest as *Wileo*, an Old English name meaning 'tricky stream', though any resemblence to the word 'wily' is alleged to be entirely coincidental. Spenser (1552?-1599) seems to have been unaware of this when he wrote in 'The Faerie Queene':

> *Next him went Wylebourne with passage sly*
> *That of his wyliness his name doth take*
> *And of himself doth name the shire thereby.*

In this passage Spenser recognised the fact that the River Wylye gave its name to Wiltshire by way of Wilton, the early name for the county having been *Wiltonscire*.

This chapter describes the valley and the associated landscapes of the river which extends for almost thirty miles from its source as the River Deverill near Kilmington to the point where the Wylye joins the River Nadder in Wilton Park. The description of such an extensive area must therefore necessarily be selective and this account of the history and the descriptions of the landscapes and the walking available in the Wylye Valley is an entirely personal selection.

One of the features which contributes so much to the charm of the valley is the contrast between the small scale of the villages which are generally situated among the shade trees along the river, and the immense scale of the open downs which enclose the valley. Around the head of the river, where it is called the Deverill, the valley is broad and the surrounding hills stand well away from the river but, after the river has become the Wylye beyond Bishopstrow, the hills tend to crowd closer and the river to be confined in a narrower valley. In his introduction to J.D.Grose's *The Flora of Wiltshire* (1957) H.W. Timperley wrote:

> In spirit these chalk stream valleys belong to the downs. They are winding ribbons of level water-meadows, with willows and elms making them leafy, between bands of more open cornfields undulating along foot slopes that steepen smoothly into the valley sides. In these valleys we are always aware of the miles of upland spaciousness surrounding them

and when writing of the Salisbury Plain villages in *English Downland* (1935), H.J. Massingham noted how 'most of the villages are warmly boxed away along the river valleys'.

The valley of the Wylye readily divides itself into three convenient sections: the Upper Wylye – also known as the Deverill Valley – from its source to Longbridge Deverill ; the Middle Wylye extending from Longbridge Deverill past Warminster to Stapleford; and the Lower Wylye, which runs from Stapleford to Wilton where the River Wylye adds its waters to those of the Nadder which flows on to join the Salisbury (or Hampshire) Avon at Salisbury.

The Deverill or Upper Wylye

The first edition of the Ordnance Survey shows the Deverill originating near Dairy Farm under Cold Kitchen Hill although it in fact rises higher up the valley. The true source is near Kilmington, but the river runs at first as a very slight stream, partly underground, until the water board enhances it from two boreholes near Kingston Deverill. From a point between Little Knoll above Maiden Bradley and Rodmead Farm a feeder stream which rises south of Little Knoll runs south to near Rodmead Farm where it turns approximately east and flows between Brimsdown Hill, Bidcombe Hill and Cold Kitchen Hill to its north, and Rodmead and Court Hills to its south, along the Deverill valley past Dairy Farm towards the Deverill villages. At this point the valley is wide and the fine ranges of chalk downland on either side are studded with a multitude of archaeological features.

In his introductory chapter 'On Roads and Footpaths' to *The Icknield Way* (1913) Edward Thomas described the footpath – a former cattle droveway

– which runs along the valley of the Deverill:

> Travellers in Wiltshire have noticed on the one-inch Ordnance Survey
> Map a "British Trackway" running W.S.W. out of the road from the
> Deverills to Maiden Bradley. A large tumulus stands in the first field,
> as if for a sign at the beginning of the track. Locally this is known as
> the "Ox Road", and is said to have been used by droves coming out of
> East and Mid Somerset... The road, in spite of its romantic Old English
> lettering, is at this point a very humble specimen of an ancient road
> and ox drove: for it goes through meadows which are low compared
> with the fine waves of down – White Sheet Downs and Maiden Bradley
> Hills – on either side of it.

This way along the valley bottom has survived as a public right of way
and remains walkable.

*Head of Deverill Valley from Court Hill with Dairy Farm (centre) and
Brimsdown Hill (background).*

The upper part of the Wylye Valley is, as described above, much more
expansive than the valley lower down. Its surrounding hills stand well back

from the river, until it funnels into a narrower configuration through the Deverill villages and assumes the true character of the Wylye, distinct from that of the Deverill, after it has turned south-east below the two great Iron Age fortresses of Battlesbury and Scratchbury near Warminster.

Brimsdown and Cold Kitchen present a scalloped hillside to the north of the Deverill, one of its great indentations being Holcombe Hole, but to the south Rodmead Hill and Court Hill offer a more constant frontage to the valley, scored by the grooves of two hollow traffic ways which run up from the valley floor to the hilltop at Court Hill. This hill is adorned with a beech belt named Court Hill Plantation which runs up the hill and over the crest, and with a gliding aerodrome which, having been discreetly sited, does not intrude upon the beauty of the valley.

Brimsdown, Bidcombe and Cold Kitchen Hills

All walkers have their favourite areas which draw them back time and time again. Such a place for me is the Deverill valley, and particularly the block of chalk downland hills situated to its north. This includes the great hills of Brimsdown, Bidcombe, and Cold Kitchen, and is bounded by the minor roads which form a triangle linking Longbridge Deverill, Monkton Deverill, and Maiden Bradley. The attractions of this area may be illustrated by the reaction of one of my walking friends upon discovering the area after coming to live in Wiltshire for the first time. He became so enamoured of the walking on Brimsdown, Bidcombe and Cold Kitchen that for a long time he walked them constantly, to the practical exclusion of all walking elsewhere.

Brimsdown Hill thrusts a promontory east towards Maiden Bradley, whilst Bidcombe is a spur of down reaching east towards Hill Deverill. Cold Kitchen Hill is a bold mass of down overlooking Kingston Deverill and Brixton Deverill. Between these three hills is Whitecliff Down, a promontory running east separated from Bidcombe by Woodcombe Bottom and from Cold Kitchen by Bushcombe Bottom. The hill above Brixton Deverill is also confusingly called Brims Down. The widely dispersed names of Whitecliff Down (between Cold Kitchen and Brimsdown), and Whitecliff Farm (between Monkton Deverill and Brixton Deverill), suggest that this entire block of downland may once have been known as Whitecliff, just as the corresponding block of downs on the opposite side of the Deverill is White Sheet. These names with their 'White' elements presumably arise from exposures of the underlying chalk on the hillsides and this district contains many chalk pits from which chalk has been excavated from these hills. A redundant shallow quarry and limekiln (828403) exists to the north of this area west of the former Charlock Hill Farm, now Lower Barn Farm (834402).

The highest of these three hills is Brimsdown which reaches 933 feet (284m), closely followed by Bidcombe at 875 feet (267m) and Cold Kitchen (845 feet: 257m). The last derives its unusual name from its Romano-British midden mound. All of these hills, which are some of the highest in Wiltshire, provide extensive views over the surrounding countryside: Brimsdown and Cold Kitchen across the Deverill Valley to the splendours of White Sheet Downs, to Rodmead and Court Hills and beyond to the distant hills of Dorset. Brimsdown also offers oblique views of the abrupt Long and Little Knolls above Maiden Bradley to the south-west, to Alfred's Tower on Kingsettle Hill on the Somerset border, and to the remnants of Selwood Forest around Stourhead. To the south-east are the wooded hills above Fonthill Gifford and East Knoyle. Bidcombe, which was in the early-19th century the subject of a long romantic poem entitled 'Bidcombe Hill' (1809) by Francis Skurray, faces north over the Longleat estate towards Frome and Westbury.

This countryside contains many monuments from the distant past, mainly the round barrows (tumuli) of the Bronze Age although there is a Neolithic long barrow on Cold Kitchen Hill. A Romano-British building – possibly a temple – formerly occupied a site at the settlement on Whitecliff Down (838388). The Cold Kitchen 'midden' (833388) or rubbish pit has over the years yielded rich artefacts which suggest that the Iron Age and Romano-British settlements which existed in this bleak and exposed position were prosperous sites.

Roman Roads

Two Roman roads cross the area, having probably forded the Deverill between Kingston Deverill and Monkton Deverill (at 851373). The lost section of the Roman road from Poole and Badbury Rings to Bath, researched by my late friend G. Bernard Berry for *A Lost Roman Road* (1963), probably ran north from this ford, having crossed the downs from Willoughby Hedge (868335) and run to the west of Keysley Farm. It probably continued north-west over Cold Kitchen through Woodcombe Farm (845392), east of Whitley Copse (842397), and half a mile west of Rye Hill Farm. There are few signs of it on the ground apart perhaps from a short hundred and fifty yard kink of west-to-east footpath (842398) immediately north of Whitley Copse at the east end of Bidcombe Wood which may be a surviving stretch of this road.

The more important 'Lead Road', which gets its name from the fact that lead was transported along it very soon after the Roman Conquest from the Mendip mines to the south coast, probably also forded the Deverill at the same ford east of Kingston Deverill, having run west from Great Ridge Wood and over Pertwood Down (where it is identifiable) and descended to the ford

Above: The Roman ford east of Kingston Deverill.

Below: Possible lost stretch of the Poole to Bath Roman road east of Bidcombe Hill (at NGR 842398).

immediately past Monkton Deverill. After fording the Deverill it would have run on west, probably along the line of Whitepits Lane, but then there is a problem. Did it rise on to Cold Kitchen and follow the high ground, or did it follow the lower ground south of Cold Kitchen past Dairy Farm (830377)? The sharp rise to over 900 feet (274m) to follow the ridge along Whitecliff Down and Brimsdown Hill for little over a mile before descending the western promontory of Brimsdown would be illogical were it not for the existence of the Romano-British settlement on Cold Kitchen which it may have served. The solution may be that the road followed the low ground but threw out a side loop to serve the Cold Kitchen Hill settlement which returned to the main line west of Brimsdown, but we shall probably never know for certain which of the alternative routes the Lead Road followed after fording the Deverill.

Overlooked from Brimsdown is Newmead Farm (819381), the birthplace of Edmund Ludlow (c1617-1692), the Parliamentary general in the Civil War who signed the death warrant of Charles I. He was a local landowner and Member of Parliament. Even before the outbreak of war, his father had the temerity to suggest in Parliament that the king was not fit to reign. Having strenuously opposed the king, Ludlow then fell out with Cromwell and spent the latter part of his life in exile at Vevey in Switzerland where he wrote his memoirs which provide one of the most authentic original sources of information on the Civil War.

Towards its west end the hilltop of Brimsdown is crowned with many gorse bushes which are a haunt of yellow-hammers, and buzzards are now commonly seen soaring above these hills, as elsewhere in the Wiltshire downlands.

In early times the villagers of Horningsham used to resort in numbers to Tom Hole – north of Brimsdown and west of Bidcombe – for frumenty celebrations. Frumenty was the fruits of hulled wheat boiled in milk. It derived its name from the Latin *frumentum* meaning corn. These hilltop celebrations may have been a survival from the fairs and markets which are believed to have been held on these hills from early times, perhaps as early as the Romano-British period.

Norse Traditions in the Deverill Valley

At Hill Deverill Sir Henry Coker, a lord of the manor who had an evil reputation and died in 1736, was alleged to haunt with his spectral hounds the grounds of Manor Farm beside the Wylye to the south-east of the village. This ghostly hunt, which is also said to have been seen at the tumulus known as Guns Church (891372) on Pertwood Down between the A350 and Pertwood

Wood, may be a survival from Norse mythology of Woden's hunt which persisted for long in English folklore. Woden, also known as Odin, was the supreme Norse god, the god of war who was believed to lead his phantom host across the sky. The *Anglo-Saxon Chronicle* for 1127 records how 'after February 6th many people saw and heard a whole pack of huntsmen in full cry', and the Old English people continued to regard Woden as the leader of a wild hunt of lost souls.

The Vikings had been very active in this area and other Norse traditions seem to have lingered here. As recently as Victorian times fair haired people at Hill Deverill were called 'Daners'.

The extensive earthworks south-west of Hill Deverill (at 866403) suggest that there has been some resettlement and that the village was formerly more closely related to its church near Manor Farm which has now become redundant and is converted to a dwelling.

A little over a mile east of Monkton Deverill are the Pertwood Down 'Celtic' field systems which cover an area of about three hundred acres west of the A350. The Roman road runs below these prehistoric fields. Although a footpath crosses Pertwood Down a little north of these field systems, their impact is greatest when they are seen from a distance, preferably in low slanting sunshine, from the road which runs south-east from Monkton Deverill towards the A350 over Pen Hill, or from the A350 itself north of Lower Pertwood.

The Middle Wylye past Warminster

Over its stretch south of Warminster the Wylye Valley loses some of its rural attraction as the river turns from running north through Longbridge Deverill and Crockerton in a wide loop past Warminster to run south-west from Bishopstrow. Within this loop of the river is found the wetland nature reserve of Smallbrook Meadows (876444) beside the Wylye's tributary stream the Were on the outskirts of Warminster. At Bishopstrow, St Aldhelm's staff is said to have been miraculously changed into an ash tree, *trow* being Old English for tree.

Beyond Bishopstrow the Wylye regains its attraction as it passes below the massive Iron Age fortresses of Battlesbury and Scratchbury which occupy the heights on the south-west edge of Salisbury Plain. The former fortress is appropriately named since it is situated at the edge of the Salisbury Plain military training ranges on the left (north-east) side of the Wylye Valley. The river now runs through the water meadow systems of Norton Bavant and Heytesbury, north of Sutton Veny and Tytherington.

The Middle Wylye

This middle section of the Wylye Valley has attracted the approbation of two discerning and well-travelled writers in William Cobbett (1763-1835) and W.H. Hudson (1841-1922), and we are fortunate that the valley has survived much as they saw it. Any valley that the irascible Cobbett described as 'very fine in its whole length', as 'singularly bright and beautiful', and as 'one of the prettiest sights that my eye ever beheld', must have a great deal to commend it. Cobbett was here on his *Rural Rides* in 1826. About eighty years later Hudson – another great traveller in southern England – fell under the spell of the Wylye Valley in 1909 when gathering material for his Wiltshire classic *A Shepherd's Life*. Hudson was captivated and more than a little bemused by the 'special attractions' that the valley came to hold for him.

Water Meadows

Throughout the entire length of the Wylye, particularly between Boreham and Wilton but to a lesser extent on the Deverill, there are many visible signs of the former water meadows which existed along the river. These take the form of countless derelict sluices, hatch gates and channels. Water meadows probably originated in a primitive form in very early times, but the practice of 'drowning' the meadows was perfected in the 17th century.

Old Rectory from footbridge at Upton Lovell.
Note undulations of former water meadows.

John Aubrey tells us that 'The improvement of watering meadows began at Wylye, about 1635,' although the name 'Water medowe' had appeared at Mere as early as 1585 and the 1631-2 survey of the Pembroke estates contain many references to 'water meads' and 'wet meadows'.

The water meadows that exist throughout the length of the Deverill and the Wylye – particularly the latter – were a man-made system by which water from the river was conducted in a controlled way over the low-lying riverside meadows to provide an early flush of grass for animals to graze.

The meadows were first ridged and furrowed. River water controlled by sluices was then introduced along carrier ditches which followed the ridges, and when these overflowed water flowed over the slopes, known as 'panes', and into drainage ditches in the furrows along which the water was returned to the river. The silt-bearing waters of the chalk stream induced an early flush of grass (the 'early bite') at the time in early spring when the hay stock was exhausted. This practice of 'floating' the meadows was controlled by a skilled man known as a 'drowner'. Water meadows continued to be used until the introduction of improved grasses and artificial fertilizers in the 19th century provided a cheaper way of obtaining early grass for the sheep which were such an integral part of Wylye Valley husbandry.

Norton Bavant to Heytesbury

William Cobbett, who as a boy had lived for a time lower down the Wylye Valley at Steeple Langford, considered this part of the valley around Norton Bavant and Heytesbury to be:

> the brightest, most beautiful, and of its extent the best of all. Smooth and verdant downs, hills and valleys of endless variety as to height and depth and shape; rich cornlands unencumbered by fences; meadows in due proportion, and those watered at pleasure; and lastly the homesteads and villages, sheltered in winter and shaded in summer by lofty and beautiful trees; to which may be added, roads never dirty and a stream never dry.
>
> *Rural Rides*, 1826

Cobbett considered Bishopstrow and Norton Bavant to be 'one of the prettiest sights my eyes ever beheld', and he took a particular liking to a farm near Bishopstrow which must have been Middleton Farm, situated betwen Battlesbury and Scratchbury near the site of the deserted village of Middleton (907446) immediately south of Middle Hill.

On the opposite side of the river lie the two villages of Sutton Veny and

*Ruined church of
St. Leonard, Sutton Veny.*

Tytherington. The 'Veny' element in Sutton Veny is really 'fenny', and reflects its marshy situation. This village has two churches, a Victorian one at its centre and a delightful ruined Norman one down a lane at the extreme east end of the village (908415). During the Great War a four-mile long military railway was run west from Heytesbury station, along the south bank of the Wylye and north of Sutton Veny village to east of Eastleigh Woods, where there were extensive camps. It then continued south of Southleigh Woods to Longbridge Deverill Camp, situated between Southleigh Woods and the river. Tytherington is a fine little dispersed village with a tiny early church about which Hudson tells the story of a dog which was inadvertantly locked in for three months and survived by licking condensation from its walls.

At the large village of Heytesbury lived the archaeologist William Cunnington (1754-1810) who collaborated with Sir Richard Colt Hoare (1758-1838) in investigating the archaeology of Wiltshire in the early-19th century. He is buried outside the north wall of the church under a flat inscribed grave slab. Heytesbury House was the home for the latter part of his life of the celebrated poet Siegfried Sassoon (1886-1967). After being highly decorated for valour in the Great War Sassoon offended the authorities by campaigning against what he believed to be deliberate prolongation of the war and only escaped official retribution by the exertions of his influential friends. Sassoon lived at Heytesbury as a slightly reclusive country gentleman who played cricket, fished and hunted, wrote poetry, entertained many of his fellow writers, and gained for himself a local reputation as an erratic car driver, a fact which prompted one landowner to sign his roadside pond THIS POND IS PRIVATE after Sassoon had driven his car into it several times.

Over the Middle Wylye the surrounding landscape is almost as impressive

as that of the Deverill Valley, although here the villages, by virtue of their sheer quality, assume as great an importance as the landscape as the down-land here crowds in on the river valley. It would be difficult to find anywhere in a four-mile stretch of countryside four small villages to equal in quality Knook, Upton Lovell, Sherring-ton, and Stockton, all of which provide good bases for walking the Wylye Valley and its ad-joining downlands.

Heytesbury church from near Tytherington.

Knook

One of the most attractive villages in the Wylye Valley is Knook, a tiny village situated on the east bank of the River Wylye between Heytesbury and Upton Lovell. Its name is probably derived from a Celtic word meaning hillock. It was *Cunuche* in Domesday. By the early 14th century the two manors at Knook were held by Lord Lovel of Wardour under the overlordship of the Earl of Gloucester, although in the late 14th century only one manor is recorded as being then held by Sir John Lovel.

Today all the buildings at Knook lie east of the Wylye, most of them in close proximity to the river. There is a small but interesting church dedicated to St Margaret which is largely Saxon-Norman transitional, although reconstructed in 1882. Its south doorway with its tympanum carved in low relief to represent two animals and interlaced tendrils is distinctly Saxon-Scandinavian in feeling and suggests the possibility of a pre-Norman Conquest date for the church. The alacrity and vigour with which the Normans erected their substantial buildings in the newly-conquered England

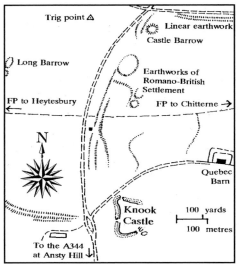

– not merely their great cathedrals but their many manor houses and parish churches – in remote backwaters such as Knook, never ceases to amaze. The carving here at Knook is less vigorous than the similar tympanum at Little Langford further down the Wylye.

Near the church is a fine small manor house with a porch, dated 1637, and stone four-light mullioned windows. It stands very near the river. In 1910 P.H. Ditchfield commented (in *The Manor Houses of England*) on 'the old manor-house of Knook, which has weathered many a storm and is now much dilapidated and liable to fall into decay. It is a good example of a late Tudor house, and is worthy of preservation'. At about the same time W.H. Hudson described Knook Manor in *A Shepherd's Life* as derelict, dirty, and neglected tenanted by a poor working man'. Its rent of 18 pence (7p) a week prompted Hudson to suggest that it was 'probably the lowest-rented manor house in England'. It is a pleasure to record that, when I last saw it in 1996, Knook manor house had been restored and was well looked after.

Knook provides a good example of a trend that occurred in many villages of early origin of moving away from their early beginnings on the high downs to the valley bottom in later times, having moved down to its present position in the valley since prehistoric times. The Iron Age and Romano-British settlements were in the hills on Knook Down, two and a half miles north-east of the present village (around 962444) at a height of about 620 feet (189m). They consisted of many dwellings associated with long linear ditches and the fortified Knook Castle earthwork (960440), a slight fortress dating from the Iron Age. There is also an earlier Neolithic long barrow (956446) and a number of Bronze Age tumuli indicating a presence on Knook Down from very early times. Here we have the Iron Age and Romano-British settlements on high land some distance from the ultimate riverside site of Knook village. Mention of Knook in Domesday and its transitional Saxon-Norman church suggests that the move to the valley probably took place in Anglo-Saxon times.

There is also decisive evidence that Knook has declined in size since medieval times. A map dated 1774 reveals that common field systems at Knook were located north-east of the A36, extending from the north flank of Knook Horse Hill almost to Willis's Field Barn (947436), and straddling the A344 Chitterne road which existed at that time. The shrunken nature of Knook is discussed in *Wiltshire Archaeological Magazine* (Volume 86, 1993). Finds suggested that the 13th century settlement at Knook extended from the river to the A36 at West Farm (941421) and consisted of two settlement areas, one around the church and manor house, the other immediately south-west of the A36 and linked to the former by a sunken lane lined with buildings along the line of the present road from the A36 to Knook. Andrews and Dury in 1773 showed buildings along the entire length of this road, but some had disappeared by the time (c1820) of the first Ordnance Survey. The split nature of this settlement may have been a legacy from the two manors which formerly existed at Knook.

Upton Lovell

A one mile walk south-east from Knook takes the walker to Upton Lovell, one of the many fine villages of this Valley of the Middle Wylye which stands to the east and a little aside from the river and a short distance south-east of Heytesbury. This widely-spread village provides an example of the innumerable pleasures such as those which rather mystified W.H. Hudson that may be found in this valley by taking the trouble to step aside from the main A36 road which accompanies the main line railway down the Wylye Valley and exploring its more unfrequented parts.

Upton means 'Ubba's farm', and by 1428 William Lovel owned the manor and gave his family name as the suffix to Upton Lovell. The chancel of the church dates from about 1200 and contains a recumbent effigy, probably that of a Lovel, with his head towards the nave.

The Lovels had formerly been at Wardour where in 1393 John, 5th Lord Lovel, was licenced to crenellate the castle, but the 7th Lord Lovel – another John – sided with the Lancastrians in 1460 and consequently lost many of the Lovel lands when the Yorkist Edward IV succeeded in 1461. They subsequently regained their lands and Francis, the 11th and last Lord Lovel (1456-87), was brought up with Richard III in the house of the Earl of Warwick. He was knighted in 1480, was created Viscount in 1483, became both Butler of England and Lord Chamberlain, and married Warwick's daughter Anne Fitzhugh. This Lord Lovel was a trusted friend of Richard III and remained loyal in 1485 when Henry Tudor threatened to invade to further his spurious claims to the throne. Lord Lovel was sent to secure the fleet at Portsmouth and organise the defence of the south coast, and fought bravely for Richard III at Bosworth in 1485. After the King's death on the field of battle he escaped and in 1485-6 raised a revolt in the north against Henry VII which was one of the several early risings which took place before Henry had firmly secured his hold on the throne. This revolt failed and Lord Lovel only just escaped capture at York. He fled to France and, in 1487, was involved in the Lambert Simnel rebellion for the Yorkist cause which also failed. The fate of Lord Lovel is not known. He may have been killed on the battlefield at Stoke, but a persistent story suggested that he escaped to one of his manors and hid in a concealed chamber where he died and his body was not discovered until the 1700s.

This story, which was related by Hudson in *A Shepherd's Life*, is told of both Upton Lovell and Minster Lovell in Oxfordshire. The Lovel mansion at Upton Lovell probably occupied the site of the large house with stone-mullioned windows to its semi-basement which stands a little north of Middle Farm.

Upton Lovell Mill

Upton Lovell Mill (943410), the last woollen mill to be operative in the Wylye Valley, was situated near the present wooden footbridge over the river. It was 'Upton Mill' on the 1773 map by Andrews and Dury, was mentioned by Cobbett in 1826, and in 1907 was described as 'the ruins of a great cloth factory' striking 'a strange and inharmonious note in the valley'. A 20 horse-power Boulton and Watt steam engine was installed here in 1822, and by 1833 no less than four hundred 'hands' were employed. It is difficult now to imagine in this delightful rural backwater of the Wylye Valley four hundred factory workers going to work in response to the factory hooter. Upton Mill continued to trade until it was damaged by fire in 1895 and a little later demolished. A modern house now occupies the site. An old photograph of Upton Mill which appears in Danny Howell's *The Wylye Valley in Old Photographs* (1988) shows it as an extensive mill with a huge factory chimney. Its records show that many of the factory workers lived at Trowbridge, lodged at Upton Lovell during the week, and walked the thirteen miles home at weekends and the thirteen miles back to Upton on Monday mornings before resuming work.

The public house at Upton Lovell bears the unusual name The Prince Leopold. This name is explained by the fact that Leopold, Duke of Albany (1853-84), the youngest son of Queen Victoria and known as Prince Leopold until he was created Duke of Albany in 1881, lived for a time at nearby Boyton Manor. He was a normal healthy child but became haemophiliac. The illness developed as he matured but he lived long enough to marry and

Former mill site on the Wylye at Upton Lovell.

father a son who became the Duke of Saxe-Coburg in 1900 and fought for Germany in the First World War. The Duke is also commemorated by Albany Cottages at Sherrington.

An examination of the Enclosure Map for Upton Lovell reveals that the village has shrunk since the map was made in the early 19th century. The slightly later Tithe Award Map of 1838 reveals that water meadows were then very extensive in the parish, those between the two streams of the Wylye at Upton Lovell being known as 'Mill Meadow'. Remains of the sluices of these water meadows and the corrugations created by the runnels and the 'panes' of grazing between the water-courses may be seen around the village. The ingenuity demonstrated by man in harnessing the river water to provide early grazing for his stock, to grind his corn, and to provide power for the manufacture of broadcloth, is quite astonishing. The demands on the river were such that formal agreements had to be entered into allocating certain days for flooding the water-meadows, milling corn, and driving the water-wheels of the woollen factories throughout the Wylye Valley.

Around Upton Lovell there is much delightful walking, both in and around the village and on the surrounding downs – to the north towards Salisbury Plain over Knook Horse Hill to Ansty Hill and Knook Castle, and to the south across the river between Corton and Boyton to the extensive woodlands of Great Ridge Ridge Wood (described in Chapter 10), a favourite haunt of Hudson, which are a delight at all seasons.

The great bustards that feature in the Wiltshire County Council crest formerly roamed Salisbury Plain and these downlands above the Wylye until they were shot to extinction for the table in the early 19th century. Today buzzards favour these uplands and I can recall seeing on a memorable occasion some years ago six buzzards soaring above Boyton Down, between Upton Lovell and Great Ridge Wood where these great birds are frequently seen and heard.

W.H. Hudson and 'A Shepherd's Life'

Jim Laverick of Bradford on Avon has established that Upton Lovell was the 'Doveton' of Hudson's *A Shepherd's Life*, and that the shepherd Caleb Bawcombe of the book was James Lawes (1830-1914) who lived from about 1856-62 at Upton Lovell in a cottage which has now been demolished in Scoute Lane (a little north of the railway at about 945406). It is almost certain that his employer 'Mr Ellerby' was Mr Ingram who owned the cottage, farmed Middle Farm almost opposite, and is commemorated by a memorial in the church porch and a table tomb on the stone-paved terrace immediately south of the church.

In these delightful villages of the Wylye, and especially at Upton Lovell, it is easy to imagine the image of an elderly tall and spare man with hawk-like expression and pointed beard, dressed in a cap and a Norfolk jacket with wing-collared shirt and a tie, and wheeling his bicycle and pursuing his insatiable curiosity about the residents – animal, bird and human – of this valley. W.H. Hudson was here for much of 1909, wandering the Wylye Valley whilst gathering his material for *A Shepherd's Life* and consolidating the information which he had been told by James Lawes in many conversations between 1902 and 1909 at the cottage at Silchester where the old shepherd lived out his last years in exile from his beloved Wiltshire Downs, quite unaware that he was to be immortalised in Hudson's classic book.

Sherrington

This village is seldom visited because it is by-passed by both roads down the valley. It stands entirely to the south and a little aside from the river. In Norman and early-medieval times both Sherrington and Boyton were held by the great Norman family of Giffard, many of whom were crusading soldiers and archbishops. To the west of the church, which was entirely rebuilt in 1624, is the moated mound upon which stood the castle of the Giffards. Watercress was formerly grown at Sherrington and the beds survive as the lakes which are a particularly beautiful feature of the village, the north-west end of Sherrington being particularly fine with its lake and its thatched cottages.

Beside a field path between Codford St Mary and Sherrington (at 968392) a Neolithic long barrow occupied an unusual situation beside a river. Other long barrows on or near the alluvium of the river in this area occur at Sutton Veny and Stockton.

South end of Sherrington.

Stockton

The last of the four villages at the heart of the Middle Wylye Valley that I have singled out for particular attention is Stockton, an attractive linear village which lies south of the river and displays a rich variety of architectural styles and building materials. The church is largely Norman and stands in a delightful cul-de-sac, surrounded by cottages and almshouses. Here John Topp, a London clothier, who in 1631 became Sheriff of Wiltshire and died in 1640, built Stockton House (977387), a fine Elizabethan house of banded stone and flint with fine interiors. This house is best seen from the public footpath which crosses Stockton Park from near Codford St. Mary to Stockton village. To the south-west of Stockton village stands the exquisite thatched group of buildings at Stockton Manor Farm (976384) which are passed by the footpath which runs from Stockton towards Great Ridge Wood and offers excellent walking over the beautiful downlands on the south side of the Wylye Valley.

The Elizabethan Stockton House.

All of these four villages – Knook, Upton Lovell, Sherrington and Stockton – are good bases from which to walk in and around the valley of the Middle Wylye, combining their riverside attractions with the innumerable options which they provide for walking on the surrounding downs.

The Codford villages – Codford St Peter and Codford St Mary – would be more attractive were they not bedevilled by the traffic along the A36, although that road has now been slightly re-aligned to miss the centre of Codford. Anthony Trollope (1815-1882), who invented the pillar box, often stayed at

Salisbury and his *Vicar of Bulhampton* is believed to have been set at Codford, which he knew well.

On the opposite side of the Wylye from Stockton, Fisherton de la Mere has succeeded in retaining the beauty that made it, in the words of an estate agent in 1898, 'so picturesque that artists often resort there [Fisherton] when wishing to paint truly beautiful and real country scenery'. Gotch's drawing of Fisherton de la Mere for Hudson's *A Shepherd's Life* reveals that the village has changed little since 1909. It has survived unspoiled and remains little-known, presumably because it stands aside from both the A36 and the minor road down the opposite side of the valley.

On the river at Fisherton is a fine reconstructed mill and mill house with a mill-pond which was the scene of a tragedy in August 1888 when a young couple, whose wish to marry had been opposed, entered into a suicide pact, tied themselves together, and threw themselves into the mill stream where they both drowned.

Fisherton de la Mere appears like several of the other villages in the Wylye Valley to have shrunk. Both Andrews and Dury in 1773 and the first Ordnance Survey of about 1820 show buildings extending east along the road by which the village is approached from the A36.

A fine short walk from Fisherton runs across the water meadows to Bapton, a hamlet on the opposite side of the Wylye. Bapton manor house was the home of Sir Cecil Chubb who, in 1905, bought Stonehenge when it was threatened with destruction and presented it to the nation.

Two miles north of the west end of Grovely Wood the village of Wylye is spoilt by the A36 and the A303 trunk roads. During the 1770s the several roads meeting at Wylye shown by Andrews and Dury on their 1773 map were turnpiked by the Amesbury Turnpike Trust and Wylye became a great centre of the coaching trade to and from the west. A statue standing in the river near the mill (now screened by a hedge) commemorates a coaching accident here. The principal turnpike was the main westwards road, now the A303, running west from Amesbury past Stonehenge and through Winterbourne Stoke and Wylye to Willoughby Hedge near Mere, but the other western road which diverged from this road at Stonehenge and ran through Shrewton and Chitterne to Heytesbury was also turnpiked by the Amesbury Trust, who also created turnpikes from Wylye up the Wylye Valley to Codford and down the valley to Little Langford. Although many categories of traffic were exempted from tolls, the Wylye Toll House levied charges as follows: 3 pence (1p) for a carriage, 1 penny for a pack animal, and 10 pence (4p) per score of cattle on the drove.

With the advent of the railway in the 1840s the turnpike roads declined overnight and remained in decline until the popularity of the bicycle and the appearance of the motor car revived them. Today these former turnpike roads have been converted into major A-roads which intersect at the huge and complicated road-junction which has been imposed on the Wylye Valley immediately north of Wylye village. The three Langfords – Hanging, Steeple and Little – are attractive villages standing on the minor roads aside from the A36.

The Lower Wylye Valley

At Stapleford, the village which stands opposite the point where the tiny River Till tumbles into the Wylye, the Middle Wylye becomes the Lower Wylye. Opposite this village both the river and the A36 make a sharp turn from running east to south. The splendid view up the Wylye Valley over the meanderings of the river from the A36 at this point was admired by Ford Madox Ford (1873-1939) and inspired him to write *Ladies With Bright Eyes*. Ford, who was a major literary figure of the first half of this century, founded *The English Review* in 1908.

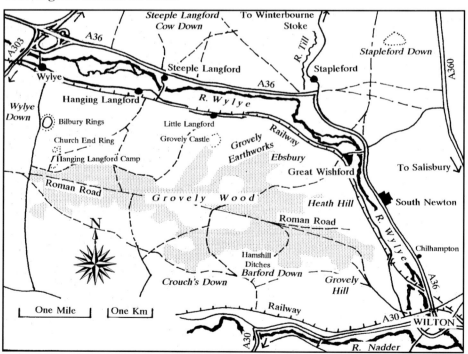

The Lower Wylye.

Thatched cottages at Stapleford on the Till.

Ralph Vaughan Williams (1872-1958), one of the greatest English composers, lived for a time at Rose Cottage at Stapleford to the east of the road south of the church. Here he composed part of his fifth symphony. Vaughan Williams, who knew Wiltshire well having been born at Down Ampney, in Gloucestershire but on the Wiltshire boundary, originally intended his ninth symphony to be a 'Wiltshire' symphony.

The best downland walking around Stapleford is over the prehistoric sites of Grovely Earthworks and Ebsbury hillfort which will be described later, in Chapter 10. Alternative walking is available to the east of the village along the Chain Drove, and north parallel to the River Till towards Winterbourne Stoke where Ford Madox Ford stayed when in this district. More walking around Stapleford is available to its north-west up the former Bristol to Salisbury coach road to Yarnbury Castle hillfort where a great sheep fair used to be held.

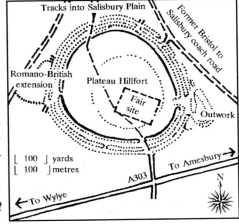

Yarnbury hillfort

Cobbett was intrigued by the little River Till at Stapleford of which he wrote:

> At Stapleford, there is a little cross valley, running up between two hills of the down. There is a little run of water about a yard wide at this time [August 1826], coming down this little vale across the road to the river [Wylye]. The little vale runs up three miles. It does not appear to be half a mile wide.
>
> *(Rural Rides*, 1825)

Cobbett then launched into one of his favourite subjects, arguing that the existence of four churches in this little vale of the Till proved that the population had once been considerably more than it was in his day.

Although the Wylye Valley defines the south-west edge of the chalk plateau of Salisbury Plain, the downlands do not entirely end at the valley. They resume to its south-west at the Great Ridge, a substantial chalk ridge capped with clay-with-flints which sustains the tree growth of Great Ridge Wood and Grovely Wood (described in Chapter 10) that crowns the ridge which runs parallel to the Wylye from near Sherrington almost to Wilton. These woods for long provided fuel for the villagers in the valley below. Other extensive woodlands associated with the Wylye Valley are the remnants of the former great Forest of Selwood of which part survives in the woods of Longleat, Southleigh and Eastleigh opposite Crockerton.

South-east from Warminster the Wylye re-enters more open terrain where, as elsewhere in Wiltshire, the bare chalk downlands adjoining the valley are in places adorned by beech trees in clumps and belts. The beech is now regarded as so typical of downland that it is generally assumed to be indigenous to the chalk. This was not the case in Wiltshire where it is a comparatively recent introduction.

Of the many references to trees in the Anglo-Saxon Charters there is no mention of beech, and in the 17th century John Aubrey informs us that there were then no beech trees in Wiltshire other than a few in Grovely Woods. In 1811 Thomas Davis, the steward at Longleat, wrote in *The Agriculture of Wilts:* 'Beech timber is not common in the county there is none grown spontaneously in Wiltshire except on the very edge of the county towards Hampshire'. It seems that the multitudes of beech trees that occupy the downs above the Wylye Valley must be attributed to the large scale plantings which were undertaken in the early 19th century. Beech will not readily regenerate on the Wiltshire chalk as it does in the Chilterns and the South Downs, except at places where clay-with-flints caps the downs as at Great Ridge and Grovely Woods.

The Woollen Industry in the Wylye Valley

It is now difficult to appreciate that the delightfully rural Wylye Valley was once a busy centre of the woollen industry which flourished in the valley for hundreds of years from about the end of the 1100s until the late 19th century. At first the raw wool was exported, but during the 14th century weaving of cloth was developed and from the 14th to the 17th centuries the woollen industry was operated as a cottage industry with the spinners and weavers working in their homes.

The fulling mills which were situated on the river then took their loosely-woven cloth and converted it into broadcloth by treating it with fullers' earth and pounding it with water-driven heavy hammers (fulling-stocks), but by the 18th century the woollen merchants were assembling their workers into the large woollen 'manufacturies' which became known as factories. At first these factories were driven by water wheels, but in the early 19th century steam power began to be introduced. The last working woollen mill in the Wylye Valley was the very large one described earlier at Upton Lovell.

The landowners of the area tended to combine farming with woollen manufacture and fine houses such as Stockton House and Stockton Manor Farm were built from the vast profits made from wool. The woollen industry of the Wylye Valley ultimately failed because of its remoteness, the insistence of the local manufacturers by continuing to produce very high quality west of England cloth when the demand was for far less expensive material, and possibly the failure of a proposal to improve transportation by running a canal up the valley from Salisbury.

The Failed Canal Proposal

In 1770 a proposal for a canal from the coast at Southampton to Salisbury was postponed as a result of the war with the American colonies. When peace came in 1783 the scheme was revived and work commenced in 1796 but soon ran into financial troubles. In 1803 war with France further impeded progress on the scheme, which included a branch up the Wylye Valley. Such a canal could have transported cheap coal to the woollen mills and carried away the finished cloth, but work on the Wylye Valley branch, which might have saved the industry in the valley, never commenced.

The Railway

The Wilts, Dorset and Weymouth Railway was constructed up the valley from Wilton to Warminster in 1856, at first in broad gauge but later converted to narrow gauge. There were stations at Wilton, Wishford, Hanging Langford, Wylye, Codford, Heytesbury and Warminster. The initial impact of both the construction and railway as a new and cheap form of transport in this secluded rural backwater must have been immense. The local people viewed the railway with some suspicion. Edith Olivier told the story of the old villager of Langford who was persuaded to go to Salisbury on market day by the train. When asked for his reaction he replied that he had never had such a dull day in his life. Unlike the carrier's cart to which he was used, the train had gone straight to Salisbury without stopping at a single pub. He wasn't going to do that again!

The Great War in the Wylye Valley

The outbreak of the First World War in August 1914 led to a great increase in traffic on the Wiltshire railway system, in particular on the Westbury-Southampton line which ran along the Wylye Valley and linked the military training area of Salisbury Plain with the embarkation port of Southampton. A great many army camps were hurriedly constructed on the Plain, including a great concentration of camps around Codford between Warminster and Salisbury. Several military railway lines were constructed to serve them, including one which ran into the downs from Codford station. Following the armistice in 1918 this railway was dismantled. The Wiltshire Record Office holds among the Warminster and Westbury R.D.C. papers (under reference G12/700/1PC) four sheets of the 1901 edition of the 6-inch map on which are plotted the Great War camps at Codford and the military hospital in Punch Bowl Bottom.

The former guardroom hut of Camp 15 (at 963402 on New Road) was converted into a dwelling called Mayflower Farm until 1995 when it was demolished and a house was built on its site. Codford station, which was near the level crossing on the minor road called Station Road which runs south-west from the A36 to Boyton village, was closed in 1957. North-west of the station, on the north side of the existing main line, was the First World War Depot. The construction of subsequent camps in the Second World War around Codford has tended to obscure the earlier First World War camps. During the Second World War the artist Rex Whistler (1905-44) was stationed at Codford and decorated a messroom which was removed to the Tank Corps Museum in London when the camp was dismantled.

The military railway left the First World War Depot (at 954402) and described a clockwise loop first north and then east. At 956403 it forked, one branch running to the south side of the A36 at 956406, the other running eastwards to cross Station Road about 100 yards south of the A36 (at 957403) and the A36 by level crossing at 960403 at the corner of Ashton Gifford Park. The park wall here shows evidence of having been adapted to accommodate

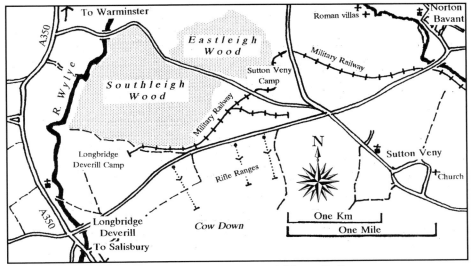

Above: Former Sutton Veny Military Railway.
Below: Former Codford Military Railway.

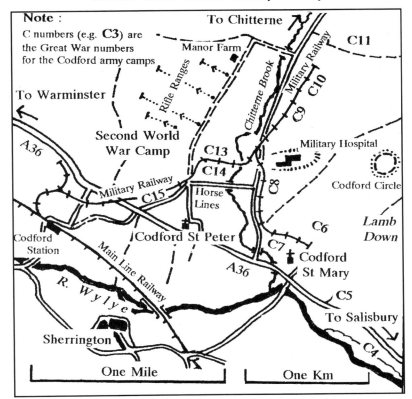

57

the railway. At this point the railway was double track. The lines continued eastwards across the site of Camp 15 where some signs remain visible on the ground, especially around the surviving Camp 15 ablutions block (962402). At about this point I was informed that the double-track lines from Codford station railway became single track and continued east-north-east down a fence line to the intersection of roads at 966404, where granite set hardstandings survive from a loading bay.

The black bitumen painted huts south of this road junction between New Road and Green Lane were the horse lines of Camp 15. From here the line turned due north to 966406 where it swung east and ran parallel to New Road a little beyond Chitterne Brook where (at 971405) it turned north-east, crossed Chitterne Road at 972407, and ran on parallel to Chitterne Road into the downs to the rail head at 977414. In the copse near the crossing of Chitterne Road are remains of walls about 3 feet high which may have been unloading platforms associated with the railway. From 972407 another branch ran south down the east side of Chitterne Road before swinging south-east to serve the military hospital in Punch Bowl Bottom and the camps at Codford St Mary, ending a little north of Codford St Mary Church.

On the east side of Chitterne Road three granite set paved yards, which are former loading bays, survive from the railway. These hardstandings have sometimes been utilised by later farm buildings. The most northerly was at Camp 10; the middle one serving Camp 9 is now used as a small timber yard, and the most southerly is at the point where the branch line to Codford St Mary crossed the bottom of the old hollow lane which runs up to Codford Circle.

The total length of the line was about two miles, of which about three-quarters of a mile was double-track. The first branch to the A36 was only 300 yards long, and the Codford St Mary branch was a little over half a mile in length. There may have been passing sidings on the single-track lengths. At the close of the war in 1918 the line was taken over by the Great Western Railway, but being of little use to them it was dismantled in 1923 or 1924. Many wooden sleepers, presumably from the military railway, may be seen in the area, including those surviving in the footbridges over Chitterne Brook.

This former military railway line has been described in detail for two reasons, first because all signs of it are now virtually lost and it has not to my knowledge been recorded elsewhere, and secondly because railway enthusiasts may care to explore the area of the former railway on foot. Such an exploration will take them into splendid walking country in the valley, sometimes known as Ashton Valley, of the Chitterne Brook which runs down through Chitterne to join the River Wylye at Codford.

Valley of the Chitterne Brook north of Codford.

Valley of the Chitterne Brook

This shallow valley was designated the Ashton Valley by the archaeologist Colt Hoare when he was excavating the Codford Down barrow cemetery (979429) here in the early 19th century, presumably from the fact that Ashton Gifford House stands towards its southern end in Codford. The valley is of interest for a number of reasons. In it stood many of the Codford military camps in the Great War, and here also ran the Codford Military Railway just described. This valley is also of interest for its profuse natural history. In it I have observed great mixed flocks of lapwing and golden plover, and here also – towards Clay Pit Hill – I have seen short-eared owls quartering the ground in daylight. On one memorable autumn day I can recall seeing an unusual association between a number of late swallows that had deferred their departure from England and early flocks of fieldfare autumn migrants. It should be mentioned that although footpaths exist in this area, no public rights of way actually follow the line of the former railway, but it is overlooked from Station Road and New Road at Codford St. Peter, from the Codford to Chitterne road, and from the footpath that runs north-east past Manor Farm from the point on New Road (966404) where the line crossed the road. This footpath, which was probably consolidated into a firm track when the Great War rifle ranges were situated beside it, provides the best access for walking in the Ashton Valley. The firing from beside this lane was west into the four butts which survive as long mounds in the east flank of the down.

In his story 'In Chitterne Churchyard' from *A Traveller in Little Things* (1921) W.H. Hudson told the amusing tale of two old village women who had come separately by rail to Codford station and had walked the four miles up the valley of the Chitterne Brook to Chitterne churchyard to attend the graves of their children. Despite being strangers they fell into amicable conversation but ended up by quarrelling about the respective virtues of their children. Hudson ends his story: 'It made me laugh and – it was too sad'.

Particularly poignant feelings about the Great War are evoked by a visit to the churchyard at Codford St. Mary. Here in the burial ground opposite the church are many graves of Commonwealth soldiers – many of them very young men from Australia, New Zealand and Canada – who, having survived the war, died while waiting to go home in the virulent influenza epidemic of 1918-19.

The Roman Conquest

The military activities of the First World War were by no means the first to take place in the Wylye Valley. During the Roman Conquest of Britain by Aulus Plautius it is possible that when Vespasian (9-79 AD) and the 2nd Augusta Legion were entrusted with the subjugation of the area that later became Wessex they may have advanced up the Wylye Valley. One of the principal reasons for the Roman invasion was to secure the lead resources of Mendip. The line of Vespasian's advance cannot now be established with certainty, but for an army advancing west from the Winchester district the Wylye Valley provides the most direct route from the Salisbury area towards Mendip which begins only about twelve miles west of Warminster. In this context, it may be significant that the 2nd Augusta, having at first struck west, ended up at Gloucester where they built a fortress to command the advance into Wales.

The Belgic tribe that occupied Wiltshire offered considerable opposition to their old enemies the Romans who had pushed them out of Gaul, and it is possible that the Romans fought their way up the Wylye Valley reducing the Belgic strongholds as they advanced and fortifying them to secure their hold on this hostile country. They would ultimately have been confronted with the great twin frowning fortresses of Scratchbury and Battlesbury opposite Bishopstrow. Outside the north-west entrance of Battlesbury was found a mass grave of men, women and children who may have been slaughtered as a result of resistance to the Romans at this time.

It is of interest to note that most of the prehistoric fortifications along the northern edges of Grovely and Great Ridge Woods – Ebsbury, Grovely

Earthworks, Bilbury Rings, and Stockton Earthworks – have revealed many signs of Roman occupation, particularly Bilbury Rings which, from the amount of Roman cavalry harness found there, seems to have been a cavalry base (this subject is discussed further in Chapter 10).

Wiltshire in 47 AD formed part of the Plautian frontier zone and by 49 AD, only six years after the conquest, we know from stamped ingots of lead that the 2nd Augusta was organising the running of the lead mines of Mendip and exporting lead along the Roman road which follows the ridge above the Wylye Valley through Great Ridge and Grovely Woods and crosses the Lower Wylye south of South Newton. In 69 AD, twenty-six years after his conquest of Wessex, after three generals had staged coups following Emperor Nero's suicide, it was Vespasian who ultimately became emperor, was deified, and continued to be the Emperor of Rome until his death.

The Lower Wylye Valley

Edward Thomas rode up the valley of the Lower Wylye on his cycle ride across the south of England for his book *In Pursuit of Spring* in 1913. As he left Wilton riding north-west along the A36 through South Newton he wrote: 'For three miles I had on my left hand the river and its meadows, poplars, willows, and elms – the railway raised slightly above the further bank – and the waved green wall of down beyond, to the edge of which came the dark trees of Grovely'. To his right Thomas described 'the edge of the Plain above the Wylye' as 'a beautiful low downland, cloven by coombs and topped by beech clumps; and where it was arable the flints washed by last night's rain were shining in the sun'.

In its course of about thirty miles from its origin as the Deverill near Little Knoll, the River Wylye has fallen about 500 feet (152m) and passed thirty village churches before joining the River Nadder east of the Palladian Bridge in Wilton Park (the many associations of the magnificent Wilton House with writers and composers are described in Chapter 11). The lower part of the Wylye Valley from Stapleford to Wilton sadly has few attractions for the walker, being so disrupted by the traffic of the A36 that it has become known locally as 'Death Valley'. As early as 1913 Edward Thomas seems to have become fed up with the main road and 'turned out of the valley at Stapleford' to cross Salisbury Plain.

The best walking in this area of the Lower Wylye is around Grovely Wood, part of the Pembroke Estate which lies north-west of Wilton and will be described in Chapter 10, but the very finest walking associated with the Wylye Valley in general is undoubtedly on the chalk downlands which overlook the Deverill Valley.

Suggested Walks in and around the Wylye Valley

8A: From Brixton Deverill over Brimsdown, Bidcombe and Cold Kitchen Hills (6 miles: map 183):

North of the Deverill the Brimsdown, Bidcombe and Cold Kitchen area is one of the finest in Wiltshire for downland walking. It is crossed by many public footpaths and a fine circular walk of about 5 miles may be taken by starting at the farm which is situated near the start of the track running north-west from Brixton Deverill (861389) to Woodcombe Farm. From this track at 853391 turn south-west and make straight for the long barrow at the top of Cold Kitchen Hill, then north-west over Whitecliff Down south of the Roman temple site to Brimsdown Hill.

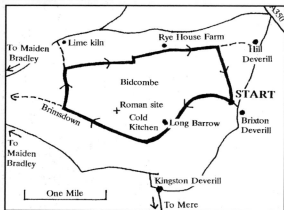

The walk may be extended by a diversion to the tumulus (816392) at the end of the promontory of Brimsdown Hill that runs west towards Maiden Bradley. Otherwise, at the first tumulus on Brimsdown (827389) turn north, drop down the embanked hollow-way through the woods and upon emerging from the woods through a gate at 827397 turn immediately east and follow the path along the north edge of Bidcombe Wood which occupies the north flank of Bidcombe Hill. After following the kink in the footpath (842398) north of Whitley Copse (is this part of the lost Roman road from Poole to Bath?) follow the ancient thorn and pond lined way (844400) east past Rye Hill Farm towards Hill Deverill but before reaching the village at 859403 follow the track southwards back to the start point near Brixton Deverill.

This circular walk, which can be started at several points on the circuit, provides many excellent views and a good feeling of the fine varied open and wooded character of this area of very special downland.

South of the Deverill Valley the walks described in Chapter 9 over White Sheet Downs and Rodmead Hill may be joined by parking on the B3092 under Little Knoll (at 804380) and walking south-east past Rodmead Farm.

From the Middle Wylye the walks south of the river in Great Ridge Wood (described in Chapter 10) may be joined from Upton Lovell where cars can be parked either at the church or at Suffers Bridge (943401) south of the village. Great Ridge Wood is then approached by walking south-west up the way past Corton Field Barn (938393). Similarly, from Sherrington (after parking immediately west of the railway at 965388), the walking in Great Ridge Wood is reached by walking south-west through Park Bottom (957373).

8B: Upton Lovell to Knook Down (6 miles: map 184):

The downs north of the Middle Wylye and the archaeological complex on Knook Down can be reached by walking north-east from Upton Lovell village past Upton Great Barrow (955423), crossing the A344 at Ansty Hill. The return route from Knook Down is south from Ansty Hill down the footpath through 962416 west of Codford St Peter and then north-west across the site of the former Codford Military Railway back to Upton Lovell.

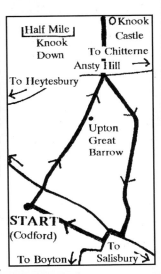

8C: Codford towards Chitterne (5 miles: map 184):

At Codford St Peter cars may conveniently be parked at 966403 and a 5 mile walk taken up the valley of Chitterne Brook, first north-east up the track past Manor Farm (970414) towards Codford Down. South of Chitterne cross the Codford to Chitterne road to Clay Pit Hill (994424) and return south-west over East Codford Down and north and west of Codford Circle to Codford.

Good walking on the Lower Wylye south of Stapleford is rather limited apart from the walking in Grovely Wood described in Chapter 10 which can be joined by parking in the beech grove above Ditchampton (at 088317) and walking north-west into the woods.

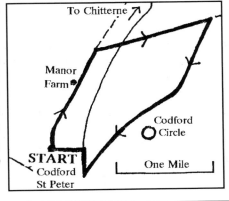

63

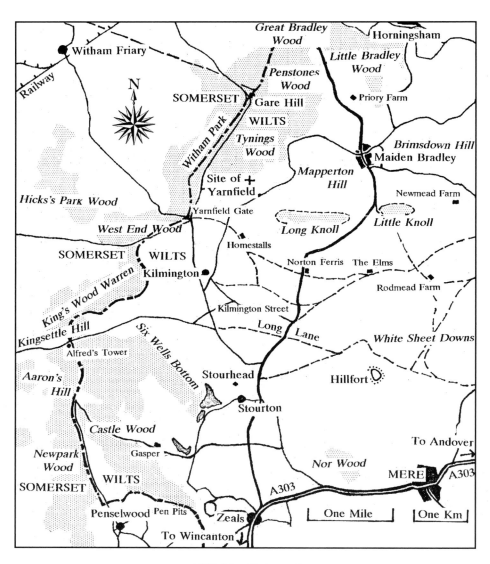

Wiltshire Selwood

9 Wiltshire Selwood and White Sheet Downs

(map Landranger 183)

Although most of the best walking in Wiltshire is in the wide upland areas of the great chalk downland that cover two-thirds of the county, the extreme south-west of Wiltshire provides excellent alternative walking. Here the broken woodlands that survive from the formerly vast Forest of Selwood follow the Somerset-Wiltshire border from near Zeals to the Longleat estate near Warminster. Associated with this Wiltshire part of Selwood is more downland walking over White Sheet Downs above the Deverill Valley, and on Long and Little Knolls above Maiden Bradley.

Wiltshire Selwood

The fragments of woodland which occupy the district where the Wiltshire chalklands merge with the claylands of Somerset are the surviving remains of the great Forest of Selwood, generally regarded as a Somerset forest although it formerly extended far into Wiltshire, as far north as Chippenham at its north-eastern extremity. As late as the 16th century Leland described Selwood Forest as 'a 30 miles yn cumpace, and streachithe one way almoste unto Werminstre and a nother way unto the quarters of Shaftesbyri by estimation a 10 miles', and yet by Leland's time the forest was much reduced from the nearly two hundred square miles it had covered in the early Middle Ages.

A forest was an area which was not necessarily wooded and was reserved by the king for his private enjoyment of hunting the wild deer. In the forests a severe code of Forest Law strictly protected the king's deer and their habitat to the great disadvantage – one might say with some justification oppression – of the human inhabitants of the forest. A forest was effectively an area of jurisdiction, and Wiltshire in early medieval times contained many forests, one of which was Wiltshire Selwood. The British natives at the time of the Roman invasion knew Selwood as *Coit Maur* (meaning 'the great forest'). By Anglo-Saxon times it was *Sealwudu*, a name made up of two Old English words – *sealh* meaning sallow and *wudu* meaning wood. Zeals at the southern end of Selwood derives its name from the same source.

Deer Parks in Wiltshire Selwood

Encroachments into the Royal Forest of Selwood by the great local landowner magnates, with or without royal permission, were a major factor in the depletion of the Forest in the Middle Ages. During the reign (1216-72), of Henry III Geoffrey of Zeals enclosed an unauthorised deer park at Zeals in Selwood. Having omitted to obtain the necessary royal licence to empark he was called to account for his actions but in 1246 was given permission for his park, situated south of Zeals House and east of Wolverton (at 795313), to remain.

Beech hanger at Heaven's Gate above Longleat, which was carved out of Selwood Forest

Deer parks proliferated in Selwood Forest. Several were created in Somerset Selwood and in 1427 Lord Stourton enclosed one thousand acres of Wiltshire Selwood into his Stourton estate and was immediately granted a licence for emparkment of part of the Royal Forest. In the mid-18th century his park was, like many former deer parks, redesigned into the exquisite example of the English landscaped garden which we see at Stourhead today.

Emparkment continued and as late as the 1570s yet another deer park was enclosed out of Wiltshire Selwood. Having acquired the Longleat estate from the Priory of St Radegund at the Dissolution of the Monasteries and completed the construction of his great house, Sir John Thynne (died 1580)

66

turned his attention to creating a park for himself by enclosing part of the forest. He then created yet another park in Corsley Park. This emparking of great areas of Selwood Forest met with strong opposition from the local gentry who had become accustomed to enjoying unrestricted hunting in the forest. In September 1580 nearly a hundred gentlemen registered their protest by entering Longleat Park with forty dogs without permission, hunting the deer and killing three bucks. The park nevertheless survived and was, like Stourhead, during the 18th century extensively redesigned (Longleat by 'Capability' Brown) into landscaped grounds as a fashionable setting for the old house.

Disafforestation continued to reduce the forest, much of it taking place during the early 17th century when Charles I, attempting to rule without Parliament, was desperate to raise funds. This disafforestation did nothing to endear Charles I to the local commoners who rioted in protest as they saw their grazing being enclosed. Enclosure and disafforestation continued to deplete the forest and today, in the greatly reduced woods of the former Selwood Forest, commercial plantations of conifers have in many areas replaced the native oak, birch and sallow. A cursory glance at the green areas of the 1: 50,000 Landranger Map (Sheet 183) reveals how fragmented and depleted are the surviving wooded parts of the former great Forest of Selwood.

The west edge of Wiltshire Selwood is defined by the Somerset-Wiltshire county boundary which follows the steep wooded escarpment facing west over the level lands of Somerset to Creech Hill and Glastonbury Tor. It runs from west of Stourton north past Alfred's Tower, through King's Wood Warren and the woods of Witham Park to Gare Hill. This escarpment effectively defines the western end of the Wiltshire chalk.

Between the Longleat estate and the meeting point of the three counties of Wiltshire, Somerset and Dorset at the lake (773312) near Bourton, the woods of Wiltshire Selwood are succesively Little Bradley Wood, Great Bradley Wood, Penstones Wood and Tynings Wood opposite Maiden Bradley. Tynings Wood is succeeded by the gap in the woodland of Kilmington Common on the Wiltshire side of the county boundary up to the Stourhead Woods which commence at Alfred's Tower at the top of the tree-shaded Kingsettle Hill. The Stourhead Woods then extend down to near Penselwood, near Bourton on the boundary with Dorset. Penselwood means the Pen (or Hill) of Selwood. The principal landowners north to south were the Lords Bath of Longleat, the Dukes of Somerset at Maiden Bradley, and the Hoare family at Stourhead.

Pen Pits

When describing Pen Pits in Volume 23 of the *Wiltshire Archaeological Magazine* (1887) Canon Jackson emphasised that even in his time they had been very much depleted:

> A mile or two beyond Stourhead... on a high ground thereabout, a large square-shaped piece of table-land, a sort of platform, the sides of which are steep declevities. On this platform stands the little scattered village of Penselwood. Pen is a very commonly-found Welsh word, meaning head, and so the name signifies, not improperly, the head of Selwood. On the slope of this platform, facing east, lie the celebrated Pen Pits... The surface of the common [Pen Common] is scooped out very irregularly into hollows or pits – some large, some small, some roundish, basin-like, others of a square or oblong shape. They are in no sort of order, but occur at intervals; some are close together, divided by a partition bank, along which you may find your way about from one to the other. The pits on this ridge are said to be spaced over 100 acres. But they did, within memory, spread also over the platform at the top, covering altogether 700 acres; a vast number having been filled in and levelled for agricultural use.

When excavating Pen Pits on Gasper Common in 1884 General Pitt-Rivers discovered that the Norman castle at Castle Orchard had been superimposed on them, proving the pits to be at least pre-Norman. Antiquarians of the past have indulged in extravagant speculation about these pits being fortifications dating from the Saxon wars which took place in this area, but Pen Pits are now generally recognised to be quarries from which quern stones for grinding corn by hand were obtained. Pottery sherds found at the site indicate a Romano-British date for these quarries.

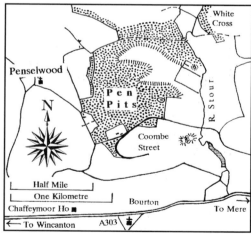

In 1934 Sir Arthur Bliss (1891-1975), the former Master of the Queen's Music, bought thirty acres of land and constructed a modern house with a studio in which he composed perched above one of the Pen Pits fifty yards from the house among the trees. Here he composed his single piano concerto, and his opera 'The Olympians' to a libretto by J.B. Priestley. Whilst Bliss was here Paul Nash (1889-1947) produced – probably in 1937 – a fine painting of Pen Pits.

At the point where the counties of Wiltshire, Somerset and Dorset meet near Bourton the headwaters of the River Stour were penned to form a mill pond for the former Bourton iron foundry. Beside this water pound, may be found with some difficulty the Egbert Stone, formerly no doubt a standing boundary stone but now lying prone and almost lost in the undergrowth.

Selwood in the Dark Ages

The several motte and bailey castle tumps which exist in the Stourhead woods across the county boundary in Somerset are an indication of the importance of this district in early-medieval times. The massive brick-built Alfred's Tower (745351) (see frontispiece) at the county boundary on Kingsettle Hill was designed by Henry Flitcroft who also designed number 10 Downing Street in London as well as many of the buildings which adorn the nearby landscaped gardens of Stourhead. It was erected by the second Henry Hoare to mark the point where he believed King Alfred had assembled his forces when he emerged from hiding in the Somerset marshes to defeat the invading Danes at Edington in 878 AD. The *Anglo-Saxon Chronicle* for 878 reads:

> And the Easter after, king Alfred with a small company built a fortification at Athelney, and from that fortification, with the men of that part of Somerset nearest to it, he continued fighting against the host. Then in the seventh week after Easter he rode to *Ecgbrihtesstan*, to the east of Selwood, and came to meet him there all the men of Somerset and Wiltshire and that part of Hampshire which was on this side of the sea, and they received him warmly. And one day later he went from those camps to Iley Oak, and one day later to Edington; and there he fought against the entire host, and put it to flight.

Wiltshire Selwood was a key area throughout the centuries between the departure of the Romans and the coming of the Normans which have become known as the Dark Ages. This name covers the period when England was being disputed first by the rival Saxons and later by the Vikings. More than two hundred years before King Alfred's campaign in 878 AD, the Saxon Kenwealh (sometimes Cenwalh) in 658 fought the Welsh (British) at a place called *Peonna*, probably Penselwood since *Penna* was the name for

Penselwood in Domesday. In the woods two miles west of Stourhead a prehistoric earthwork is sometimes known as Kenwealh's Castle (748335).

Over three hundred and fifty years later another battle took place at Penselwood when the Dane Cnut and the English King Edmund Ironside met in battle here in 1016. Cnut had become by conquest master of the greater part of England, having the previous year ravaged Dorset, Wiltshire and Somerset. Edmund Ironside was appointed King of the English to oppose Cnut. Both were young men, Cnut being twenty-one and Edmund Ironside probably in his mid-twenties. Pitched battles were at this time rather unusual as the Vikings normally raided and then rapidly made off with their booty before any concentration of opposing forces could be gathered to oppose them. The two armies marched and counter-marched and finally met at Penselwood in 1016, but the battle was indecisive and after several more battles the two kings made peace and divided England. Cnut took Mercia and the north, and Edmund Ironside settled for Wessex which then comprised the entire south of England. Shortly after this Edmund died and Cnut assumed sovereignty of the whole of England which he reigned undisputed from 1016 until his death in 1035.

Opposite Alfred's Tower on the other side of the way up Kingsettle Hill stands Jack's Castle (746354), a Bronze Age tumulus near the county boundary on the wooded scarp a quarter of a mile north of Alfred's Tower. In *The Green Roads of England* (1914), Hippisley Cox calls the barrow 'Jack Straw's Castle', but any connection between this remote Wiltshire barrow and Jack Straw, the east countryman who was one of the leaders of the 1381 Peasants' Revolt, is difficult to explain.

The west edge of Wiltshire Selwood is well served with public footpaths which criss-cross both the woods and the more open landscape of the Kilmington district at Kilmington Common. The car park opposite Alfred's Tower provides a good starting point for exploring the surviving woods which run along the Somerset-Wiltshire border.

Kilmington church is associated with a double murder which took place in 1556. John Aubrey tells the story of Lord Stourton, a member of the ancient local family, who resented the elevation of the First Lord Pembroke, a mere soldier of fortune who had been promoted to his elevated position by Henry VIII. Lord Stourton appointed a man of bad reputation called Hartgill as his steward. This man proceeded to cheat Lord Stourton out of many of his lands. A prolongued dispute followed but the disputants appeared to be living amicably, when Lord Stourton suddenly seized Hartgill and his son and imprisoned them in the tower of Kilmington church where he had them murdered. He was tried, convicted, and hanged – it is said with a silken rope out of deference to his rank – in Salisbury market place on 6 March 1556. It is said that Queen Mary sent a reprieve for Lord Stourton, who shared her Catholic faith, to his enemy Lord Pembroke but he deliberately arranged for the messenger to be delayed at Wilton and rushed off to Salisbury to ensure that the sentence was carried out.

At this western edge of Wiltshire Selwood the Roman road, along which after the Roman Conquest lead was transported by packhorse from the Mendip Hills to the coast, crossed Selwood at Gare Hill on the county boundary.

At the south edge of Tynings Wood is the site of the deserted village of Yarnfield (780384) which is accessible by public footpath but about which very little is known, I suspect because boundary changes have caused it over the years to be sometimes in Somerset and at other times, as at present, in Wiltshire.

Yarnfield Gate (768377) – *geat* in Middle English means 'gate' or 'pass' – marks the point on the county boundary where an alternative pass to Kingsettle Hill through Selwood entered Wiltshire three-quarters of a mile south-west of the deserted village of Yarnfield and near the west end of Long Knoll. The route up Druley Hill and through Yarnfield Gate became a droveway out of Somerset which continued south of Long Knoll and Little Knoll to pass through Norton Ferris, enter the head of the Deverill Valley, and run on eastwards through Kingston Deverill. The droveway survives as a public footpath which remains walkable along the valley between Long and Little Knoll and Brimsdown to its north and White Sheet Downs and Rodmead Hill to its south.

It has been suggested by C. Cochrane in *The Lost Roads of Wessex* (1969) that 'A search through south-west England for an area that represented in its communication lines every phase of history might easily be met by the square mile around Alfred's Tower'. Here the Hardway climbs out of Somerset through the woods at Kingsettle Hill and continues, marked by milestones, across the open land around Kilmington with fine views of The Knolls ahead, on to the White Sheet Downs, at first as Alfred's Tower Road and later as Long Lane and the London Drove Road.

Long Lane Drove

This way out of Somerset up Kingsettle Hill past Alfred's Tower and on to the White Sheet Downs was from earliest times the principal crossing of Selwood Forest. It passes the Red Lion Inn at Kilmington (787353) and climbs White Sheet Downs past the lime quarry which is a mass of wild flowers in

Left: Long Lane passing under White Sheet quarry.

Below: Milestone on Long Lane near White Sheet quarry with Long Knoll in background.

spring with cowslips much in evidence. Later in the year this is a fine place for orchids. Over this stretch it has become known as Long Lane. At the top of the hill near a milestone (801353) Long Lane bends to the right, passes through a Neolithic causewayed camp, and crosses the vast open landscape of White Sheet Downs as the London Drove Road. Half a mile east of White Sheet Castle hillfort (at 814346 opposite Great Bottom running up from Mere) the milestone indicating a hundred miles to London, inscribed with a 'C' and much graffitti, stands strangely isolated in the middle of the track, a fact which led Edward Thomas to describe it as 'like a traveller asleep'.

This old droveway out of Somerset and across White Sheet Downs was beautifully described by Thomas in his introductory chapter entitled 'On Roads and Footpaths' to *The Icknield Way* (1916):

It crosses the little shaded river Brue and ascends Kingsettle Hill between high banks of beech and oak and bluebell. It mounts, like a savage who does not mind being out of breath, straight up the steep wooded wall of the hill until at the top it is eight hundred and fifty feet high instead of four hundred, and takes you into Wiltshire. On the right is the huge square [actually triangular] of brick erected by one of the Colt Hoare family in honour of King Alfred... The road takes you through the remains of Selwood Forest. Now it has a fair green border, often of considerable breadth. That you are in Wiltshire there can be no doubt on emerging from the trees. For in front upon the left are those gentle monsters, the smooth Long and Little Knolls above Maiden Bradley, smooth, detached green dunes crested and fringed with beeches. Under this side of the Long Knoll is the tower of Kilmington church among its trees. Lying across the road a few miles ahead are the bare White Sheet Downs, which are to be mounted, and farther right the wooded beacons above Fonthill Gifford and East Knoyle. The road makes for a high quarry on the nearest slope of White Sheet, a little to the left of a lesser isolated hill, a smooth, wooded knoll or islet [Search Knoll]... The lane turns to climb White Sheet Hill... Looking back, the Knolls are on the right and Alfred's Tower on the left among the woods. There are tumuli on the right as the road comes clear out on the hilltop and travels between the wired fences of the downland pasture.

A little north of Long and Little Knolls is the village of Maiden Bradley. A leper hospital here became a priory of Augustinian canons, of which there are slight remains at Priory Farm (799403) a mile north of the village beside a small lake that was presumably once a fish pond. It is passed by a public footpath. The Dukes of Somerset have a house at Maiden Bradley which is now much diminished from its former grandeur. The village fountain was erected by the 14th Duke of Somerset in 1891. It is inscribed with doggerel verse including the couplet:

Drink, travellers, drink, from Bradley's purest rill,
Which, strange to say, runs quite a mile uphill.

Former line of droveway seen from White Sheet quarry, Search Knoll (left).

The Civil War and the Monmouth Rebellion

Just as the Saxon-Viking wars described earlier touched this area in the Dark Ages, so did the Civil War and the Monmouth Rebellion in the 17th century. Half a mile north-west of Horningsham and a little north-east of Little Bradley Wood is the site of Woodhouse Castle (801420). In the Civil War it was garrisoned for the king by William Arundell, a brother of Lord Arundell of Wardour, and was taken by Parliament. Subsequently it was retaken by Sir Francis Dodington who is alleged to have hanged on one tree fourteen soldiers of the garrison, an allegation which is confirmed by the fact that in June 1649 Agnes Young, the widow of Roger Young, petitioned for relief at Warminster because after the surrender of Woodhouse, in the words of the petition: 'Sir Francis Doddington (the bloody tyrant) hanged your petitioners said husband with thirteen soldiers more of the garrison'.

A mile from Woodhouse stands the great estate of Longleat which was, as we have seen (page 66), carved out of the woods of Selwood Forest by Sir John Thynne (1515-1580). Sir John, who had acquired the Longleat estate at the Dissolution, was a favourite of Protector Somerset who showered him with wealth when he effectively reigned England as Protector during the minority of Edward VI. Although sent to the Tower, Sir John survived Somerset's fall and execution and retired to live quietly at Longleat. Despite the activity at nearby Woodhouse Castle the Thynnes 'laid low' during the Civil War.

During his almost royal progress through the West Country to sound out his popularity in 1680, Charles II's illegitimate son the Duke of Monmouth passed through Maiden Bradley where he was acclaimed as the Protestant hope by the local people, on his way to Longleat where he was royally entertained by 'Tom of Ten Thousand' Thynne. When, in 1685, he made his bid for the throne of his Catholic uncle James II, most of Monmouth's recruitment took place in Somerset, but this south-west corner of Wiltshire provided some recruits, largely as a result of the activities of John Kidd, the influential former Longleat gamekeeper who, as 'Captain' Kidd, recruited in the Longleat area. He is said to have enrolled some of the Longleat retainers and many local people, to the number of about five hundred, although Monmouth's muster rolls and the records of the trials do not support this number. Perhaps some recruits had the good sense to withdraw.

'Tom of Ten Thousand' Thynne (1648-1662) – his name was an indication of his income – who had opposed James II and entertained Monmouth on his 1680 progress, was the Issachar of Dryden's immensely popular political poem 'Absalom and Architophel '(1681) directed against Monmouth which reads:

But hospitable treats did most commend
Wise Issachar, his wealthy western friend

By 1685 'Tom of Ten Thousand' had been murdered and Longleat had been inherited by his cousin Sir Thomas Thynne (1640-1714) who, although he too disliked James II and was one of the four lords who later invited William of Orange to England, refused to support Monmouth. He remained loyal to King James and was considerably embarrassed by the fact that some of his staff defected to Monmouth.

After Monmouth's decisive defeat at Sedgemoor 'Captain' Kidd, aware that he could expect no mercy after his enthusiastic recruiting activities on behalf of Monmouth, fled to the Longleat area where he had many friends. He was captured by the Earl of Pembroke, who was Lord Lieutenant of Wiltshire, on 7 July near Stourhead in a large party of about eighty rebels, and was sent to Salisbury Goal. In Pembroke's report Kidd was alleged to be the only 'Knight' created by Monmouth. No executions took place in Wiltshire after the Rebellion. Kidd was taken to Dorset and executed on 12 September with eleven other rebels at the spot on the beach at Lyme Regis where Monmouth had landed.

Mere Down Lynchets.

75

White Sheet Downs

The Forest of Selwood originally extended much farther east towards Salisbury Plain, over the area that has now become the open downland of the White Sheet Downs where only the valleys are sparsely wooded. For the purposes of this chapter the eastern boundary of the district described is taken to be roughly a line from Mere over White Sheet Downs and through Maiden Bradley and Horningsham, although an exception is made for the magnificent series of strip-lynchets situated north of the A303 and a little north-east of Mere which must be included as they are only surpassed by the lynchets above Bishopstone in North Wiltshire (described in Chapter 1 of Volume 1 North). The Mere Down lynchets extend along the sides of the coombes of Chetcombe Bottom, Aucumbe Bottom and Ashfield Bottom and are now readily accessible on foot. They are also visible from the B3095 a mile north from Mere and from the public footpath which runs south from the London Drove Road over Mere Down from 836344 to the A303.

Although Andrews and Dury do not show a racecourse on their 1773 map, we know from a description by Colt Hoare of a race-meeting in 1733 that a country racecourse formerly existed on Mere Down in the 18th century.

The grassed-over face of White Sheet quarry which probably gave White Sheet its name.

White Sheet Downs with their complex of archaeological sites of many periods provide some of the very best downland walking in a particularly remote part of Wiltshire with long views north-east to Cranmore Tower in Somerset and south into Dorset where Duncliffe Hill near Shaftesbury and Hambledon Hill are seen on the southern horizon. Immediately north of White Sheet is the great tapering shallow valley which forms the head of the Deverill Valley (see Chapter 8), running between noble ranges of hills in White Sheet Downs, Rodmead and Court Hills to its south, and Brimsdown and Cold Kitchen Hills to its north, with Long and Little Knolls and Zeals Knoll as outlying hills standing like great islands in the gap between them. Long Knoll offers a fine oblique view past the beech-crested Little Knoll into the head of the Deverill valley towards Kingston Deverill (see cover picture).

Access to White Sheet Downs is excellent, and a good walk is to be had by parking at the quarry on White Sheet (at 797350) and walking either up the macadamed droveway or up the steep undulating turf path which climbs the chalk hill above the quarry on to White Sheet Downs. Here may be found a great concentration of prehistoric field monuments – a Neolithic causewayed camp (801351), several Bronze Age round barrows, and a fine Iron Age hillfort (804346), as well as several pillow-mounds used for rabbit breeding at the foot of the hills. There is also a possible medieval deer park (centred on 810352) situated beside the milestone-lined Long Lane Drove along which from medieval times herds of cattle from the Somerset Levels were driven eastwards across south Wiltshire towards London. A little to the east of this area this droveway was recorded as the London Drove Road, and even further east beside Grovely Woods (see Chapter 10) as the the Western Drove Road. A little east of White Sheet hillfort it is possible to leave this droveway (at 811347) and by first turning north-east cross Rodmead Hill and then turning east and following a footpath over Court Hill reach towards Kingston Deverill in the Deverill Valley.

Long and Little Knoll

North of the White Sheet Downs the two Knolls called Long and Little Knoll are now both accessible to walkers. A public footpath follows the ridge of Long Knoll, and although Little Knoll (see front cover) is not crossed by a public footpath, at the time of writing (1996) the public has been granted the right to roam over the knoll under the Countryside Stewardship Scheme. John Aubrey (1626-97), the Wiltshire antiquary and writer, knew Long Knoll as a result of his friendship with Francis Potter the rector of Kilmington, and loved the extensive views from it. Both of the Knolls provide long views south across White Sheet Downs to Dorset. Long Knoll reaches a height of 945 feet (288m) and from it the views are panoramic, taking in most of the area once covered by the Forest of Selwood. From here it is possible on a clear day to see Glastonbury Tor at a distance of sixteen miles, as well as the more distant landmarks of Dorset.

Stourhead

As described earlier (page 66), in the early-15th century Lord Stourton carved a great estate out of Selwood Forest at Stourton. During the mid-18th century this estate was transformed by its new owners, the banking family of Hoare, into magnificent landscaped gardens and renamed Stourhead. In *The Englishness of English Art* (1956) Sir Nikolaus Pevsner suggested that 'the landscaped garden is the most influential of all English innovations in art', and at Stourhead we have one of the greatest examples of this style of landscape which has survived very much as it was created in the 1740s. Although this man-made artificial landscape is not appreciated by some, I believe that all walkers in this area should judge for themselves by devoting an hour or two to entering the grounds at Stourhead (which are in the care of The National Trust) and walking around the lake, preferably in an anti-clockwise direction. The anti-clockwise circuit is important as the layout and disposition of the architectural features of the grounds were arranged to create an allegory of Aeneas's journey after the fall of Troy in Virgil's *The Aeneid*, as depicted by Claude Lorraine in his classical landscapes.

When I think of the landscape of Wiltshire Selwood the delights enjoyed on innumerable visits to the gardens at Stourhead come to mind, as do many memorable walks in the woods and glades near the county boundary. I also recall the bluff west end of Long Knoll seen from near the site of Yarnfield deserted village, the fine view of White Sheet Downs seen from Long Knoll – and conversely the long mound of Long Knoll seen from White Sheet Downs – but particularly I recall many long walks over the austere upland landscape of the White Sheet Downs, over countryside described by Timperley and Brill in their *Ancient Trackways of Wessex* (1965) as 'one of the loneliest downland walks in Wiltshire'.

Stourhead: the Pantheon.

Suggested Walks in Wiltshire Selwood and over White Sheet Downs

9A: From Alfred's Tower through the woods to Gare Hill and Yarnfield
(9 miles: map 183):

One of the many woodland walks in Wiltshire Selwood that can be taken from the car park opposite Alfred's Tower (747353) is north and north-east through the woods of King's Wood Warren to Druley Hill. After walking north-east up the road at Yarnfield Gate on the county boundary continue north along the path parallel to the road, through Witham Park Wood to Gare Hill (780401). From Gare Hill the walk back to Alfred's Tower is south between Penstones and Tynings Woods, through the site of the deserted village of Yarnfield (779385), and back past Grange Farm and through Yarnfield Gate (768377). From here the way back is by the outgoing route down Druley Hill and through King's Wood Warren. This walk (of which the early part is actually in Somerset but closely following the Wiltshire boundary) amounts to about 9 miles. There are many deer in these woods, buzzards soar above them, and in spring the woods are a mass of bluebells.

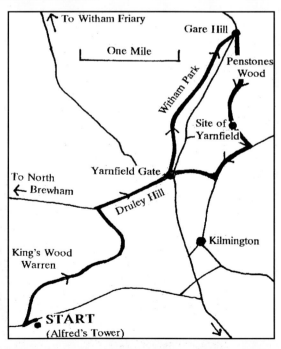

79

9B: Long Knoll and Little Knoll (6 miles: map 183):

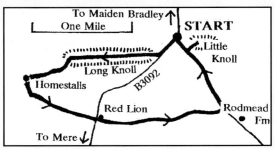

Long Knoll and Little Knoll may be incorporated in a walk by parking a car between them at the point (803380) where the driveway to Rodmead Farm leaves the B3092. After a short walk south-west down the B3092, branch right on to the footpath which leaves the road at 801377, pass through a small copse on the col by which the road passes between the Knolls. This path takes the walker after a short climb along the ridge of Long Knoll. At its western end the steep descent from Long Knoll to Homestalls (778373) is reminiscent of the descent from the west end of Martinsell Hill over Giant's Grave to Oare (see Chapter 6 of Volume 1). From Homestalls the return route is south-east then east following the droveway which runs from Yarnfield Gate through Norton Ferris past The Elms (802366) to near Rodmead Farm. From a little north-west of this farm (812637) continue north-west along the drive from Rodmead Farm to the start point. If a mile is added for a short stroll on the very steep Little Knoll (which is now accessible under the Countryside Stewardship scheme) on the way back to the start point, the total length of this walk is about 6 miles.

9C: White Sheet Downs (4 to 6 miles: map 183):

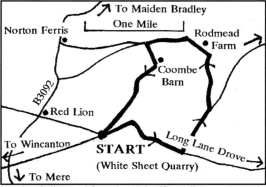

The austere open uplands of White Sheet Downs may be traversed by parking in the car park near the former quarry (797350) a mile east of the Red Lion at Kilmington and walking either north-east up Long Lane tarmacadamed way or east over the stile and up the steep grassy footpath above the former lime quarry to the downs. Long Lane may then be followed for about half a mile eastwards towards Mere Down, at 811348 turning north east and then descending into the valley past Rodmead Farm and west then south past Coombe Barn (806363). White Sheet Downs are regained by walking south-west up the shoulder of the down. If the walker turns as described back from Rodmead Hill this walk amounts to 4 miles, but if the option is taken of extending the walk to Court Hill above Kingston Deverill this will extend the walk by about 2 miles. The walk may also be extended into a much longer walk by adding to it Walk 9B over Long and Little Knolls described above.

9D: Mere Down Lynchets (4.5 miles: map 183):
The open countryside of the Mere Down lynchets may be incorporated in a walk commencing at Mere (where there are car parks), passing east of Manor Farm in walking north up the gentle incline on to White Sheet Downs. From White Sheet the Long Lane droveway is followed east over Mere Down, crossing the B3095 and at 826344 turning south to walk above the lynchets and then cross the A303 to Burton. From Burton one of the footpaths west may be taken from Burton to Mere.

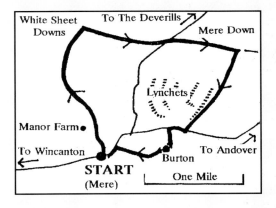

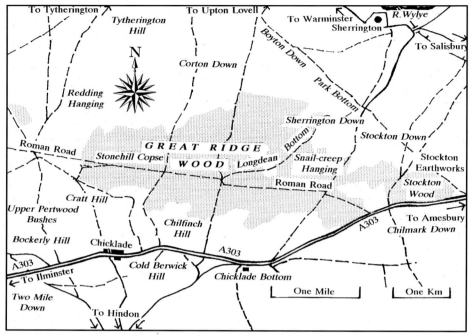

Above: Great Ridge Wood; Below: Grovely Wood.

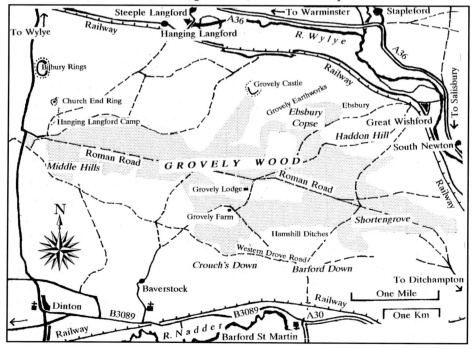

10 Great Ridge and Grovely Woods

(map Landranger 184)

Much of the really memorable walking in Wiltshire is provided by the wide open downlands for which the county is celebrated where woods are intermittent and sparse. A contrast is provided by Great Ridge Wood and Grovely Wood which crown the long ridge of clay-with-flints capped chalk downland which occupies the watershed between the Rivers Wylye and Nadder, running down to near Wilton in south Wiltshire.

Great Ridge Wood

Great Ridge Wood was early in the present century a haunt of the writer W.H. Hudson (1841-1922) who in his classic Wiltshire book *A Shepherd's Life* devoted much of his chapter headed 'The Shepherd as Naturalist' to this wood, which he described as:

> an immense wood, mostly of scrub or dwarf oak, very dense in some parts, in others thin, with open, barren patches, and like a wild forest, covering altogether twelve or fourteen square miles – perhaps more. There are no houses near, and no people in it except a few gamekeepers: I spent long days in it without meeting a human being. It was a joy to me to find such a spot in England, so wild and solitary.

We too may enjoy similar pleasures to Hudson by spending long days 'roaming about in this endless wood', for it survives today as wild and solitary as when he knew it in 1909. A glance at the Ordnance Survey map of Wiltshire reveals that Great Ridge Wood is one of the largest woods in Wiltshire, comparable with Savernake Forest and more extensive than either Grovely Wood or the Wiltshire part of Cranborne Chase, and yet it is comparatively little known. Hudson in fact greatly overestimated the size of Great Ridge Wood which, if the ancillary Stockton Wood which lies immediately to its east is included, extends for only about four miles west to east and an average of only about one mile from north to south. Although in the main a long solid

range of dense downland, it is indented from its north-east by a particularly attractive wooded coombe called Longdean Bottom (943365) along which runs a public footpath with above it the intriguingly named Snail-creep Hanging (945361).

West edge of Great Ridge Wood south of Tyther-ington.

Snail-creep Hanging

This fascinating place-name which is applied to the triangle of hanging woods between Stony Hill, Longdean Bottom, and the Roman road through the Great Ridge, merits a short explanatory digression for *The Place-Names of Wiltshire* (1939) fails to mention this unusual place name. The 'Snail-creep' element arises from the many large Roman edible snails *Helix pomatia* which proliferate here and may be seen in great numbers after rain, and a 'hanging' – or 'hanger' – is a wood which appears to hang on a steep slope. The name 'hanger' is common in Hampshire but is less usual in Wiltshire.

This explanation for the 'snail' element of the name is confirmed if Longdean Bottom is walked on a damp summer evening after rain when a profusion of Roman snails will probably be seen. This snail, which is easily the largest British land snail  being almost two inches (50mm) long, is the edible snail – the escargot – which is generally eaten in France and is sometimes farmed in England for the French market. It is in fact native to the calcareous soils of southern England and was not introduced by the Romans as its name implies. The name probably arose because the Romans relished it, and it is therefore interesting to notice that these snails proliferate so near the former Roman road through Great Ridge Wood. We know from Tacitus that, although they carried mess tins and cooking pots, Roman soldiers seldom ate meat. Their food was extremely simple, consisting largely of corn supplemented by bread, fruit and vegetables. Oyster shells and mussel shells have been unearthed at many Roman sites, and it is probable that edible snails were also eaten as shells of edible snails were found at the Roman town at Silchester.

The possibility that shells of snails could be valuable indicators on archaeological sites was first realised by the geologist Clement Reid in 1896 when he advanced the idea in the *Proceedings of the Dorset Field Club* (xvii, 69). Different species of snail thrive in widely differing conditions of dampness and in different habitats such as woodland, open down, or scrub. From their presence it is therefore reasonable to infer the conditions of climate and habitat obtaining at the time that the snails were buried. Mollusc evidence has been used in dating many sites including Stonehenge, and from evidence provided by snail shells we are aware that in the late Bronze Age and the Iron Age the climate became drier than it had formerly been and approximated to the climate of today.

Geoffrey Grigson, the Wiltshire-based poet, critic and historian, used to tell an amusing story about the Roman snail. He was showing an American visitor over the Neolithic causewayed camp of Knap Hill above the Vale of Pewsey and explaining to his incredulous listener the extreme age of the camp. Grigson explained how part of the earthwork was a Roman extension to the much older existing camp. The American bent down, picked up a snail, and said sarcastically, 'And I suppose this is a Roman snail'. 'And it was, it was,' cried Grigson exultantly.

In addition to Snail-creep Hanging and Longdean Bottom already mentioned, the map of Great Ridge Wood reveals several other interesting place-names which include Musseldean Copse (908366) at its extreme west end and Chilfinch Hanging (927356) towards its south edge, Chilfinch being an archaic name for chaffinch.

The great delight of Great Ridge Wood is the undulating nature of its terrain, its mixture of dense woodland and open clearings which was noted by Hudson, and the long views that are obtained from its margins, to the north across the Wylye Valley into Salisbury Plain, and from its south edge to the distant Win Green Hill on the Dorset boundary.

Wildlife in Great Ridge Wood

When describing the great woods of Wiltshire – Savernake, Collingbourne, Longleat, Cranborne Chase, Fonthill, Great Ridge Wood, Bentley and Grovely Woods – in *Adventures Among Birds* (1913), W.H. Hudson deplored the 'sense of something wanting' in these woods which he defined as the lack of the great birds of prey due to the predations of the keepers. Now, largely due to Hudson's efforts in founding the Royal Society for the Protection of Birds, sparrowhawks and kestrels are regularly seen in Great Ridge Wood, the sharp 'mew' of the buzzard is often heard, and the great birds are frequently seen soaring above the tree canopy.

Great Ridge Wood provides shelter for a great many wild deer which are best watched in the very early morning when they are feeding and do not anticipate the presence of humans. Although deer are generally timid creatures it is advisable to be cautious when approaching male deer during the rutting season in September and October when the males are in prime condition and are jealous of their females. The author can recall being confronted one late autumn afternoon by an aggressive large buck near Chilfinch Hanging, one of the remoter parts of Great Ridge Wood.

The place-names Park Bottom (953375), to the north of the wood, and High Park (940354) to its south are possible indications that here the great Norman family of Giffards of Boyton and Sherrington, who owned a castle at the latter village, had a deer park in early medieval times.

Nightingales are heard in season, and owls are sometimes heard eerily calling here during the daytime. The many clearings in the woodland make Great Ridge Wood especially good for wild flowers and butterflies. In spring it becomes a haze of bluebells, and I can recall on a July day in the glorious summer of 1976 leading a natural history society on a walk in Great Ridge Wood and finding the glades of Longdean Bottom absolutely teeming with butterflies, mainly silver washed fritillaries, more butterflies than I have seen before or since. The dominant tree species is oak, often dwarfed, with birch and ash also present in great numbers.

Adders are to my knowledge present in Great Ridge Wood. Many years ago I accidentally trod on an adder sunning itself in a rut in Longdean Bottom. The snake understandably struck at my leg and then rapidly snaked off into the undergrowth at the foot of Snail-creep Hanging. The adder (or viper) is the only venomous snake native to England and as such has been greatly persecuted, although tales of the danger arising from adder bite are greatly exaggerated. Its reputation probably originated in countries where people went about unshod. The venom of the adder rarely kills humans in this country and over the last sixty years there have been only about twelve fatalities in Britain from adder bites, for the adder is not a danger to man if left alone.

Archaeological Sites of Great Ridge Wood

Although it is the larger and wilder wood, Great Ridge Wood is less richly endowed with archaeological sites than is Grovely Wood, but it contains some earthworks of uncertain date. By far its most impressive archaeological site is Stockton Earthworks (970362), a large late Iron Age settlement defended by a surrounding bank and ditch and extending over about sixty acres, backing on to the woods and associated with extensive prehistoric field systems. These earthworks are situated immediately north of Stockton Wood, an outlying part of Great Ridge Wood. Stockton Earthworks appear to be an unfinished hillfort which was adapted by the Romans, for excavation has revealed that the settlement was occupied throughout the Romano-British period.

The *Victoria County History of Wiltshire* (Volume 11) suggests that Stockton Earthworks was a farming village 'but may have been additionally a posting station and even a minor market'. It stands on the way which runs directly south-east from Corton in the Wylye Valley over Boyton Down (947383) and along the shoulder of Park Bottom, over Stockton Down (960370) and through Stockton Earthworks on its way south-east, joining the Roman road near Down Farm on Chilmark Down (at 978353), and perhaps runs on south-east towards the Teffont villages. This is probably a very ancient

prehistoric way that was adopted and Romanised by the Romans as an approach road to Stockton Earthworks. A local resident once told me that this way, as it rises from Sherrington Pond (957373) in Park Bottom up Stockton Down towards the Romano-British settlement, was formerly known locally as the 'Market Way'.

The most obvious walk in Great Ridge Wood is along the drive which approx-

The way to the Roman settlement at Stockton Earthworks (in trees on horizon) running over Boyton Down.

The drive which follows the Roman road along the ridge through Great Ridge Wood, looking east.

imately follows the line of the Roman 'Lead Road' from Mendip towards the coast. This is in my estimation a rather boring walk as the drive is gun-barrel straight and level, and the trees completely shut out the long views that would otherwise be obtained from the ridge over the surrounding downlands. My criticism of this Roman road for its straightness leads me to ask whether the Romans ever became dissatisfied with their rigidly straight roads and longed for more interesting winding ways such as those followed by their predecessors. Walking this Roman road along the Great Ridge is in my opinion best avoided, or at least made more interesting by adopting the infrequent options of diverting from it along some of the footpaths which cross it.

The wildest part of Great Ridge Wood is on its south side towards its west end, around Chilfinch Wood (925353) where the broken edge of the wood offers long views south across the Fonthills and the Nadder Valley to the distinctive tree-crowned Win Green Hill which stands exactly due south and eleven miles distant on the Wiltshire-Dorset boundary.

Up to about the middle of the 19th century, when herds and flocks came on the hoof to the great stock fairs, the way south from Corton Field Barn (938393) south across the Great Ridge and over Chilfinch Hill, and the parallel way a little to its west, must have been followed by herds and flocks moving on the drove to the great fairs that were held on Cold Berwick Hill immediately south of the A303 above Hindon. Both of these droveways survive as public rights of way.

West of Great Ridge Wood the Roman road running east from Pertwood Down passes through an ancient intersection of ways (897365). Here the Roman road is no longer a public right of way, but four other rights of way and a parish boundary meet at this point and offer good walking, north towards Sutton Veny and Tytherington, or south past Upper Pertwood and over Upper Pertwood Bushes and Bockerly Hill towards Chicklade and Hindon, with the option of entering Great Ridge Wood at Stonehill Copse.

The best approaches to Great Ridge Wood on foot are from the Wylye

Valley to its north, either from Upton Lovell or Tytherington, or from Stockton past Manor Farm to Stockton Earthworks. The wood may alternatively be approached from the A303 to its south, although walking on the south side of the wood is marred by the proximity of the busy traffic on the A303 which runs along this side of the Great Ridge. Walking to the south of Great Ridge Wood does however offer the option of combining walks in the woods with an exploration of William Beckford's Fonthill Estate with its magnificent Palladian gatehouse (933327) and its fine lake. From Fonthill the approach to Great Ridge Wood is north beside the lake and under the gatehouse, along the minor road from Fonthill Bishop to Chicklade Bottom (938343) where the A303 is crossed. The woods are then approached up the long incline which enters Great Ridge Wood at 948354. This would have been W.H. Hudson's approach to Great Ridge Wood when he was staying at Fonthill Bishop researching *A Shepherd's Life* in 1909. It has a particular poignancy for me as it is the route that was followed by the poet Edward Thomas (1878-1917) on

his last walk in England from East Hatch to his camp at Codford one bleak January evening in 1917 before embarking the next morning for France and death on the Western Front.

To wander in Great Ridge Wood is invariably a joy, due largely to the fact that although several public footpaths cross the woods it is unusual to meet another walker here. In my experience of this wood extending over some thirty years, almost every visit brings with it something memorable, and I never tire of visiting Great Ridge Wood.

Right: Gatehouse at Font-hill Bishop and the lake.

Grovely Wood

Immediately east of Great Ridge lies its sister, Grovely Wood, which similarly straddles the ridge between the Wylye and the Nadder over a length of about six miles from the copse known as Dinton Beeches (007348) at its west end almost to Wilton where the two rivers meet.

Beech avenue in Grovely, looking east.

Grovely Wood contains two trackways which follow the ridge through the woods, both of which provide good walking. One of these ways approximately follows the line of the former Roman road from Mendip to Old Sarum along a drive which follows the crown of the ridge at an altitude from about 574 to 656 feet (175 to 200 metres). In the western part of Grovely this Roman road practically coincides with the open drive along the ridge through the woods, but east of Grovely Lodge the drive diverges from the line of the Roman road and runs a little to its north. The other old milestoned trackway roughly follows the broken south margin of Grovely Wood at a lower level. It was formerly known as the Western Drove Road.

Roman Road through Grovely

Lead was of great importance to the Romans both in its own right for use as pipework and bath linings, and for its silver which could easily be separated out by the cupellation process. The Roman road through Grovely is sometimes known as the 'Lead Road' because the discovery of date-stamped lead ingots beside it further to the east establish that lead from the Mendip mines was being transported along it to the south coast ports for export to the Continent within a few years of the Roman Conquest.

After following the ridge eastwards through Great Ridge Wood the Lead Road crossed The Bake and continued along the ridge through the woods to near the east end of Grovely where it seems to have veered slightly to the left of its former line in making for the Roman station at Old Sarum (*Sorviodunum*). Most of the line of this road is plotted on the Ordnance Survey, generally a little north of the long straight ride through the woods. Where visible, its *agger* (the Roman word for the embankment) is about eighteen feet wide.

The precise line by which the road crossed the Wylye Valley east of Grovely Wood is now uncertain, although it probably forded the river a little south of South Newton. Its line here was almost certainly lost when Wilton became an important place in Saxon times and travellers along this road tended to leave the Roman line towards the east end of Grovely and divert to Wilton by descending by way of The Hollows (084324), known by the Saxons as *Wudu weg* meaning 'the way of the wood'. After leaving Wilton the Saxons then took a separate line back to rejoin the Roman line at Old Sarum, probably by way of a ford at Stratford-sub-Castle. It was this diversion to Wilton which contributed to the Roman road across the Wylye Valley being abandoned and its line lost.

In 1955 the Roman road was excavated a little west of Grovely Lodge and found to consist of a sub-base of chalk rubble and clay-with-flints and a seven inch (175mm) surfacing of flint. The fact that the road was metalled on the dry high ground suggests that a heavier construction would have been used on its valley crossing, which makes its complete disappearance here all the more surprising. Its materials may have sunk into the soft valley floor of the water meadows, or more probably have been quarried for building materials – or both.

The Hollows at Ditchampton, the former Saxon way to the east end of Grovely Woods.

91

Grovely as a Royal Forest

In the Middle Ages Wiltshire was a land of forests and Grovely Wood is a survival from one of these forests. In early times it was Grovely Forest, a forest being a royal hunting ground subject to Forest Law which protected the wild deer for the king to hunt to the great disadvantage of the local people. Grovely was, as the *foresta de Gravelinges,* the only forest to be mentioned in Wiltshire Domesday in 1086. A 1589 drawing shows a wooden paling fence around Grovely Lodge at the centre of Grovely Wood with stags within a rectangular enclosure, suggesting that Grovely Lodge was then surrounded by a deer park.

Grovely is narrower and more indented than Great Ridge Wood, and early maps reveal that it was formerly very much more extensive than it survives today, extending almost to the gates of Wilton. In Norman times it would have been used as a royal hunting forest from Old Sarum Castle four miles to its east, and possibly also from Stapleford Castle two miles to its north where Waleran the Venator, the chief huntsman to William I and Ranger of the New Forest, owned land. Access to Grovely from Old Sarum may have been along the now lost stretch of the Roman road across the Wylye Valley. The approach from Stapleford would have been by way of the fords over the Wylye at Little Langford and Wishford.

The Civil War

During the Civil War the clubmen – the peace movement of local people who opposed both factions in an attempt to curtail the war and limit the depradations of the warring armies – assembled in great numbers in Grovely Woods where they presumably felt secure from interference. The House of Lords Journals reported that the Clubmen assembled 'wearing a badge of white ribbon, and armed with fowling-pieces, pikes, halberts and clubs, rendezvoused at Grovely, Warminster, Stonehenge and Whiteparish to the number of 4000 men'.

Another connection of this district with the Civil War existed at the fine village of Dinton, two miles south of the west end of Grovely. Here was born Edward Hyde, 1st Earl of Clarendon (1609-1674), the moderate royalist statesman who wrote the impartial *The True Historical Narrative of the Rebellion and Civil Wars in England,* which was not published until 1702-4, long after his death. Clarendon was the father of Anne Hyde who married James II and was the mother of two queens, Queen Mary and Queen Anne. Hyde's House, which stands a little west of Dinton church, was originally a Tudor building but was reconstructed in the Wren style. Dinton is also worth visiting for Lawe's Cottage, a 17th century stone building which was the

Edward Hyde, Earl of Clarendon, born at Dinton.

birthplace of Henry Lawes (1596-1662), the court composer who set Milton's 'Comus' so effectively that Milton considered that he had matched poetry to music to perfection. Henry Lawes collaborated in the writing of the first English opera 'The Siege of Rhodes' (1656). He had a younger brother, William Lawes (1602-1645) who was a composer of masques and songs, became musician to Charles I, and died fighting for the king at the siege of Chester in the Civil War.

By ancient custom the people of Wishford to the east of Grovely Forest and of Barford St. Martin to its south had the right to gather fuel from Grovely. In the 19th century its landowner the great Earl of Pembroke, tried to suppress the right but some village women chose to stand up for their rights, ignored the great Earl's edicts, and persisted in gathering their wood. They were sent to prison but when the matter was examined the peoples' rights were confirmed and have never subsequently been challenged.

Along the ridge occupied by Great Ridge Wood and Grovely Wood the chalk downs are overlaid with clay-with-flints. The botanist Mr J.D. Grose noted that in Grovely 'The shrub layer is particularly rich and varied', and John Aubrey recorded that 'the deer of Grovely were the largest and fattest deer in England, but some doe affirm the deer of Cranborne Chase to be larger than Grovely'. A considerable deer population still remains in Grovely Wood where wild deer can frequently be seen today.

Grovely Wood is, like Great Ridge Wood to its west, a delightful place to walk at all seasons. Being nearer to Wilton and Salisbury, it tends to be rather more frequented than Great Ridge Wood – especially towards its eastern end – but is extensive enough to absorb many visitors. The straight drive which runs along the ridge through Grovely and is partly macadamed is monotonous and makes rather dull walking, although its beech-lined eastern end is sufficiently majestic to make it comparable with the more celebrated Grand Avenue of Savernake Forest. The monotony arises, as with the drive along the ridge through Great Ridge Wood, from its severe straightness and the blocking out of the potential views by the dense woods.

Western Drove Road

Far more interesting is the old track which follows the south edge of Grovely from near Dinton Beeches at the west end of Grovely, over Middle Hill, Crouch's Down and Grovely Hill, and plunges down The Hollows into the Ditchampton end of Wilton. This way, which was furnished in the 18th century with a surviving set of milestones (don't bother searching for the one above Baverstock as this one is missing), became part of the old Western Drove Road running east from the Somerset Levels where cattle were fattened before being driven 'on-the-hoof' towards London. Beside the droveway was an inn called 'The New Inn' (026335), shown by Andrews and Dury in 1773 a little west of the missing eight miles from Sarum milestone above Baverstock.

Drove road leaving the south edge of Grovely Woods looking west above Chilmark.

Salisbury was a great market for cattle-dealing in former times, and from here some of the drove cattle continued towards London, while others turned southwards towards the coast to be slaughtered and salted down as salt beef to provision the navy. This old way along the south margin of Grovely Wood with its milestones (which were described by Edward Thomas in his diary in 1917 as 'Old milestones lichened as with battered gold and silver nails') provides excellent walking with good views to the south across the Nadder Valley to the Nadder-Ebble ridge opposite.

The Archaeology of Grovely Wood

As in Great Ridge Wood the south facing slopes south of Grovely Wood between the woods and the A303 are covered with 'Celtic' field systems. Among them is Hamshill Ditches (at 058332) on Barford Down, a complex of ditches, Iron Age enclosures, and field systems. Two small circular enclosures of the 'spectacle' type are here linked by causeways to a linear ditch, with to their east many hut platforms of the Romano-British settlement with multiple banks and ditches and approach roads. Excavation has turned up many Romano-British artefacts. A footpath runs south out of the woods, crosses Hamshill Ditches, and continues down to Barford St. Martin in the valley.

Another footpath which provides long panoramic views north across the Wylye Valley into the heart of Salisbury Plain follows much of the northern edge of Grovely Wood where a succession of Iron Age sites – Ebsbury, Grovely Earthworks, Grovely Castle, Hanging Langford Camp, Church End Ring, and Bilbury Rings – adjoin the woods. The fact that nearly all of these native sites were adopted by the Romans led me to suggest earlier (in Chapter 8) that during its advance west under the future Emperor Vespasian, the 2nd Augusta Legion may have thrust up the Wylye Valley immediately north of Great Ridge and Grovely Woods through the territory of the Belgae towards Mendip and its mineral wealth that was to be exploited very soon after the Roman Conquest was completed.

The Belgae

During the last phase of the Iron Age, from about 25 BC to 43 AD the Belgae had begun to appear in England, first as refugees from the Roman conquest of Gaul and then as colonists. The Belgic culture had developed in Northern Gaul in the area that is now Belgium. The Belgae were a riverside farming people who used the heavy wheeled ox-drawn plough with coulter and mould board which enabled them to plough the heavy loams and clays of the valleys. They also used iron spades and axes.

They tended to found states to replace tribal groupings, and urban capitals such as *Verulaneum* (St Albans), *Calleva* (Silchester), and *Camulodunum* (Colchester). Initially they settled in south-east England, but from about 50 BC, following the threat posed by the abortive expeditions to Britain of Julius Caesar in 55 and 54 BC, they expanded westwards until by about 10 to 25 AD Wiltshire had been occupied by the Belgic leader Commius. This expansion led to the conversion of a number of hillforts to Belgic use and the construction of new forts.

As a result of their tendency to change their settlement locations to lower ground the Belgae practically abandoned the established practice of building hillforts on isolated hilltops and introduced fortified sites which were often defended settlements surrounded by quite slight earthen ramparts and backing on to woods which offered facilities for guerrilla warfare and provided refuge, fuel, and building materials for their huts. This practice was described by Caesar in *De Belli Gallico* (V: 1-23): 'The Britons call a place a town when they have fortified a thick wood with a rampart and a ditch, and to such places they are wont to retreat when they want to avoid an inroad of the enemy'.

Ebsbury, Grovely Earthworks and Stockton Earthworks (the latter at the north edge of Stockton Wood adjoining Great Ridge Wood and described earlier in this chapter in my account of that wood) are all examples of this practice. Ebsbury (065354) is very fine, being both a hillfort and a Romano-British settlement with 'Celtic' fields adjoining. The discontinuity of its ramparts may be the result of its residents ploughing down their defences during the *Pax Romana* and moving to the east of their former hillfort.

Grovely Earthworks (060356), together with Ebsbury, form a crescent one mile long around the north and east edges of Ebsbury Copse at the north-east corner of Grovely. Between Grovely Earthworks and Grovely Castle a beautiful deep coombe cuts into the north face of Grovely. Grovely Castle (048358) appears to be a small unfinished hillfort enclosing thirteen acres on a spur of open down overlooking the Wylye above Great Wishford. The Belgic period was so short that many Belgic works remained unfinished at the time of the Roman Conquest, and at Grovely Castle the ramparts are slight and those on its north side seem never to have been completed. It must surely be coincidental that Grovely Castle, Old Sarum (138327), and Stonehenge (123422) form a perfect equilateral triangle, that Grovely Castle, Stonehenge and Sidbury hillfort (217505 near Tidworth) stand in line, and that when that line is extended south-west it passes through Castle Ditches hillfort (963283) above Tisbury.

Three miles west of Grovely Castle are Hanging Langford Camp, Church End Ring, and Bilbury Rings. Hanging Langford Camp (013352) is a defensive settlement covering forty-five acres which was known as *Eorthburg* in 940 AD. It is connected by a ditch with Church End Ring (013356), a pear-shaped enclosure at the head of Stancombe with its ditch inside the bank suggesting a ceremonial rather than a defensive purpose. The name arises from its former use for non-conformist meetings.

Bilbury Rings (010362) is a normal hillfort standing to the north of Grovely Woods on a spur of down south of the Wylye Valley. It is circular in shape, encloses seventeen acres, and now has a farm at its centre. Much Roman cavalry equipment was found at Bilbury which was presumably used as a cavalry base. The panoramic views from Bilbury rings across the Wylye Valley and into the vastness of Salisbury Plain are memorable and serve as a reminder that Iron Age sites are almost always worth visiting for the views that they offer and for the exhilaration that is felt from being at these high prehistoric places.

North edge of Grovely Woods from near Bilbury Rings.

Great Ridge and Grovely Woods are very fine places to walk. They offer diversity of terrain with a combination of open downlands and dense woodlands with many open glades, and they provide a change from the open downland walking that is the great glory of walking in Wiltshire. These woodlands are delightful both in the first flush of spring when the fresh beech foliage is still a translucent vivid green and the woods are carpeted with bluebells, and in autumn when the trees – particularly the beeches – become a riot of colour. All this in addition to the archaeology, the profusion of wildlife, the magnificent views from the margins of the woods, and the fact that these woods are both vast and little frequented.

We should consider ourselves fortunate that Hudson's discovery, expressed in *A Shepherd's Life*, that 'It was a joy to me to find such a spot in England, so wild and solitary' is as relevant today as when he wrote in 1909.

Suggested Walks in Great Ridge and Grovely Woods

10A: Great Ridge Wood from Park Bottom (5 miles: map 184):

Experience of the attractive and varied terrain of Great Ridge Wood is obtained by following a 5 mile triangular walk from near the former Sherrington Pond in Park Bottom (957373). This was 'Upper Cross Ways' on Andrews and Dury's 1773 map from the number of paths that intersect at this point and offer many options for walkers. This point is accessible by car and here cars may also be parked. The suggested route runs first south-west along Longdean Bottom which used to be far

more open than it is today, for the trees have encroached in the last thirty years. One of the best views of Great Ridge Wood – a view that gives an appreciation of the vast extent and density of this great wood – is obtained from the heights of Stony Hill (952365) which may be climbed as a short diversion south-east from Longdean Bottom (from 947367). From this hill a great panoramic view is obtained westwards over the treetops of Longdean Bottom and other parts of Great Ridge Wood, and up the steep tree-clad slopes of Rowdean Hill to the contrasting bare grasslands at the top of Corton Down. Such a view provides us with some understanding of why prehistoric man feared dense forests and chose to live on the more open hilltops. The way along Longdean continues under Snail-creep Hanging and climbs the long fairly gentle incline to meet the Roman road (at 931361) near the centre of the wood. From this point the walk may be extended south-west to Chilfinch Hill at the south edge of the woods. Otherwise, from this intersection at the very heart of the wood the way lies north through the woods past the point (934377) where the way suddenly bursts out of the woods and magnificent views open up over rolling downland west toward Long Knoll and Little Knoll. The walk continues north to Corton Field Barn (938393) at the head of Boyton Bottom. From here the way back to Park Bottom is down the gently inclined Romanised way over the open downland of Boyton Down. This fine triangular walk may alternatively be joined at Corton Field Barn by parking well to the north of Great Ridge Wood at Suffers Bridge (943401) at the south end of Upton Lovell and walking south into the wood.

In these dense woodlands of Great Ridge and Grovely – particularly the latter – it is preferable to try to achieve variety and obtain varied views by incorporating some of both the north and south fringes of the woods into a walk, remembering that the south edges gets the sun but can be exposed, and that the north edges of the woods are shaded from the sun but provide shelter from the prevailing wind.

10B: East end Grovely Woods from above Ditchampton (9 miles: map 183):

Such variety may be achieved by parking a car at the beech clump (088317) west of Ditchampton and walking north-west then west along the Western Drove Road along the south edge of Grovely, remembering to keep an eye open for its milestones. Above Baverstock (036332) take the public footpath north-east across the woods past Grovely Farm and Grovely Lodge,

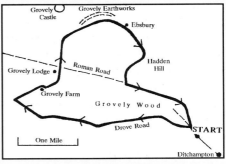

then follow one of the footpaths north to the edge of the woods and follow the north edge of the woods past the prehistoric sites of Grovely Earthworks, and Ebsbury hillfort and over Hadden Hill, enjoying the splendid views to their north across the Wylye Valley into Salisbury Plain. The return is east and south along the drive back to the start point at the west end of Grovely.

10C: West end Grovely Woods from Dinton Beeches (7 miles: map 183):

After parking near the west end of Grovely near Dinton Beeches (006350) (unfortunately a convenient small car park here has recently been removed), walk east along the droveway along the south edge of the woods watching for the milestones along the way (the former milestone above Baverstock is the missing one of the series). Above Baverstock (at 036332) turn north-east

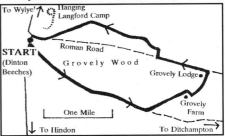

and pass Grovely Farm and Grovely Lodge. At the latter turn west along the approximate line of the Roman road, now a drive through the woods. Take one of the paths to the north edge of the woods and then follow the footpath which runs along the north edge of the wood past Hanging Langford Camp back to Dinton Beeches.

99

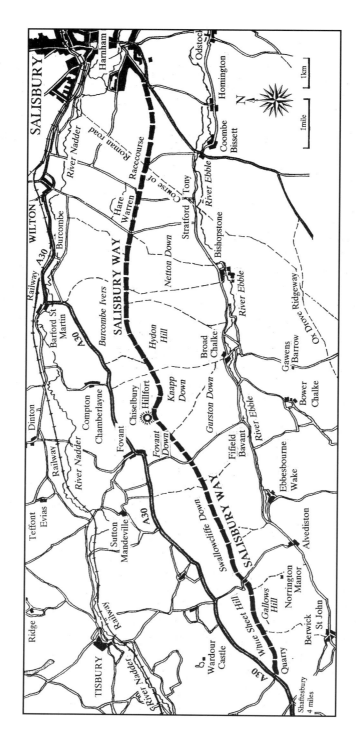

The Salisbury Way

11 The South Wiltshire Ridgeways:
The Salisbury Way and the Ox Drove

(map Landranger 184)

The south of Wiltshire is crossed by three rivers with between them three ranges of chalk downland radiating from Salisbury which form the watersheds between the Rivers Wylye, Nadder and Ebble as they run down to Salisbury to unite with the River Bourne to form the Salisbury Avon. These ridges, which provide truly glorious elevated walking with exhilarating long views over south Wiltshire and into Dorset, are all followed by old communication routes. The Great Ridge is followed by the Roman road and the Western Drove Road already described in Chapter 10. The next ridge, between the Nadder and the Ebble, is followed by the Salisbury Way, and to the south of the Ebble between that river and Cranborne Chase runs the Ox Drove Ridgeway. The Salisbury Way and the Ox Drove and their associated countrysides are the subject of this chapter.

The Salisbury Way

This, the more northern of the two ridgeways, was described by C. Cochrane in *The Lost Roads of Wessex* (1969) as 'In many ways one of the most remarkable stretches of road in England'. The Salisbury Way rises out of the A30 valley road near Donhead five miles east of Shaftesbury, climbs through a quarry at White Sheet Hill, and follows the Ebble-Nadder ridge for thirteen miles past Chiselbury Camp and Salisbury Racecourse south of Wilton before descending into Harnham, a southern suburb of Salisbury. In the Anglo-Saxon charters it was designated both 'broad highway' and *herepath* (military or long-distance road). Later it became known as both the Shaston Drove – Shaston being the ancient name for Shaftesbury used until recent times by local people – and as the Salisbury Way. This ridgeway would have been of particular importance during the Middle Ages when people were required to be religious and all who could afford it went on pilgrimage to holy places. The Salisbury Way was then the principal communication route between Salisbury – in 1377 on the basis of its taxpaying population the sixth town in England – and Shaftesbury, which had been a sanctified place since

101

980 AD when the body of King Edward the Martyr was brought there for burial after his murder at Corfe.

In its rise through White Sheet quarry the Salisbury Way is deeply hollowed between massive white banks of gleaming chalk. Over this sharp climb it is difficult to imagine coaches staggering up – or even down – the steep hill, but soon it bursts into the open and attains high ground at a height of 794 feet (242m) on White Sheet Hill. This high downland can be very exposed, a fact emphasised by the lengthy account of a bleak Easter Sunday spent on White Sheet Hill included by W.H. Hudson in Chapter XII of *Afoot in England* (1909). Over its first section from White Sheet to Middle Down the Salisbury Way is at its highest, but the height of the way then gently declines throughout its course. It is crossed by a succession of no less than eighteen prehistoric cross-ridge dykes in its progression along the Ebble-Nadder ridge to Salisbury, short lengths of dyke that are evidently not defensive earthworks and are now generally believed to have defined territorial boundaries between adjoining prehistoric estates or farms.

The Salisbury Way running east from White Sheet across Gallows Hill.

At the east end of White Sheet Hill the way passes north of Gallows Hill (954243) and Norrington Manor which will be described later in this chapter. The Salisbury Way was described by William Stukeley in his *Itinerarium Curiosum* (1724):

The road from Wilton to Shaftesbury, called the Ten Mile Course, is a fine ridge of downs, continued upon the southern bank of the River Nader, with a sweet prospect to the right and left, all the way, over the towns and the country on both sides: a traveller is highly indebted to your lordship [Lord Pembroke] for adding to his pleasure and advantage in reviving the Roman method of placing a numbered stone at every mile, and the living index of a tree to make it more observable.

Lord Pembroke's milestones anticipated the turnpiking of the Salisbury Way which took place in the late-18th century, and Stukeley's mile trees explain the 'Mile Trees' shown along the Salisbury Way by Andrews and Dury on their 1773 map of Wiltshire. The alternative name of 'Ten Mile Course' arose from Lord Pembroke's use in the 17th and 18th centuries of the Salisbury Way for horse-racing, when it became known as 'The Race'. Two principal horse races were run, originally for a prize silver bell presented by the second Earl of Pembroke for which in 1630 a gold cup was substituted. These two races were a fourteen-mile race from Whitesheet Hill to Harnham Hill, and a shorter four-mile race from the place known as 'The Start' opposite Broad Chalke to Hare Warren. The idea for the mile trees placed by the Earl of Pembroke along the Salisbury Way may have developed from mile markers connected with his horse-racing activities.

This stretch of the turnpike was worked by a highwayman called 'Cunning Dick'. In Gurston Wood (017277), a little south-west of Chiselbury Camp and five or six miles east of Gallows Hill, there existed some years ago – and it may still exist – an oak tree about a hundred yards south of the turnpike on the edge of the wood with a large staple to which Cunning Dick used to tether his horse while awaiting his victims.

The Vale of Wardour

North of the west end of the Salisbury Way, opposite White Sheet Hill and towards the west end of the infant River Nadder as it runs north from Donhead St Andrew, lies the interesting area sometimes known as the Vale of Wardour which provides excellent walking associated with the Salisbury Way. The scenery of the Vale of Wardour and the Nadder Valley with their rich meadowlands and their multitudes of trees contrasts with the bare austerity of the high downs which carry the Salisbury Way along the ridge to their south. The Vale of Wardour is an area of Greensand containing deposits of Purbeck and Portland stone. Through it run the tributary streams that spring up around the Donheads and combine near Wardour Castle with the River Sem coming from Semley to form the River Nadder.

Near the Donhead villages it is believed that the Abbess of Shaftesbury had a grange at Lower Berry Court (911236), formerly Bury Court, two miles from Win Green and beside Ferne Brook, one of the headwaters of the Nadder. Lower Berry Court is almost on the line of the Roman road as it runs north from near Win Green through the Donheads, a name which evolved from 'down-head'. Donhead Hall (904238), south of Donhead St. Mary, was built by Sir Godfrey Kneller, a grandson of the painter, and is consequently 'Donhead Hall: Goy Kneller Esq' on Andrews and Dury who mixed up Donhead St. Mary and Donhead St. Andrew on their 1773 map of Wiltshire.

At Wincombe near Donhead St. Mary the celebrated historian Sir Arthur Bryant lived from 1956 to 1963 in a modest Regency house situated in a 360 acre estate in a secluded coombe where he had spent childhood holidays staying with an aunt and uncle. He loved Wincombe, which he described as 'that little corner of earth where Wiltshire joins Dorset and the infant Nadder rises'.

By tradition the older part of the rectory at Donhead St. Mary was, like the Hospitaller Commandery at Ansty three miles to its north-east (see later), a halting-place for pilgrims to Shaftesbury who, after descending to the valley from the Salisbury Way through White Sheet quarry, would have passed within a mile of the rectory through Ludwell on the present A30.

Two miles north-east of the Donheads lies the Wardour estate containing the now-ruined Old Wardour Castle (938263) which underwent a siege in the Civil War, and New Wardour Castle (928269), a vast Palladian mansion built towards the end of the 18th century which was for long a school but has

Above left: Ruin of Old Wardour Castle (right) with its 18th century pavilion (left).
Below left: New Wardour Castle, built 1769-1776.

104

recently been converted into flats. Wardour was the seat of the Catholic Arundell family whose sumptuous Georgian chapel stands beside their house. In this chapel the celebrated classical guitarist Julian Bream (born 1933) likes to record because of its fine acoustics. The area around Old Wardour Castle (which is now in the care of English Heritage) offers magnificent walking in wooded country with several lakes which was until the 18th century laid out as deer parks with separate parks for red deer and fallow deer, but was subsequently landscaped.

A little north-east of Wardour the large village of Tisbury is rather distant from the Salisbury Way but is mentioned for its literary associations. To the east of Tisbury, at the manor house of Chicksgrove on the Nadder, was born and lived Sir John Davies (1569-1626), the poet and lawyer. His poetry was very highly regarded in the Elizabethan age. He attracted the attention of James I who made him Solicitor-General of Ireland and later Attorney General and Lord Chief Justice. Davies was also the founder of the Society of Antiquaries. Another literary association at Tisbury is with Rudyard Kipling (1865-1936) who was frequently here when his parents, who are buried in the churchyard, lived at Tisbury. If Tisbury is incorporated in a walk, on no account should the medieval farm group of gatehouse, farmhouse and tithe barn at the former Abbess of Shaftesbury's Place Farm to the east of the village be missed.

East Hatch Farm (926284), a mile south-west of Tisbury, was at the time of the Great War rented by the writer Arthur Ransome (1884-1967), and here his friend the poet and critic Edward Thomas spent his penultimate night in England visiting his six-year old daughter Myfanwy before returning to camp at Codford and embarking for France where he was killed near Arras in April 1917.

At Ansty, east of Wardour and two miles south of Tisbury, the Knights Hospitallers had from the year 1211 a Commandery, probably on the site of Ansty Manor. Their establishment included a hospice which may sometimes have accommodated travellers along the Salisbury Way which runs three miles to its south. Richard II confirmed the possession of 'the Hermitage of Ansty' and of 'eight dwellings built thereon' to the Knights Hospitallers. Hospitals originated as places which offered hospitality to travellers, particularly to pilgrims. Some remains of the Hospitallers' Commandery, including the large barn-like building that was probably a guest house, may still be seen near the church at the south end of the raised lake that makes Ansty such an attractive village. When, from 1208 to 1214, the whole of England lay under a papal interdict as a result of the quarrel between King John and the Pope, Ansty would have been one of the few churches open for worship in the district as the Monastic Orders of the Knights Templar and the Knights Hospitallers were exempted from the interdict.

White Sheet from the Salisbury Way south of Ansty.

The Salisbury Way (cont.)

Shortly before crossing the minor road from Ansty to Alvediston, where the former prime minister Sir Anthony Eden is buried in the churchyard, the Salisbury Way enters one of its few wooded stretches as it passes through a beech copse on Middle Down above the dramatic hairpin descent of the cross road to Ansty. The dramatically steep great scoop in the down facing north towards Swallowcliffe and Castle Ditches hillfort is Swallowcliffe Down. In the 1930s an enterprising local farmer indulged in some free advertising when, by the use of sulphate of ammonia to promote grass growth, he inscribed on the wall of the down D R I N K   M O R E   M I L K in huge dark green letters against the pale turf of the almost vertical face of Swallowcliffe Down. This slogan caused a great outcry but nothing could be done to prevent its annual reappearance until the effects of the chemical wore off after several years. After crossing Swallowcliffe Down the Salisbury Way continues over Sutton and Fovant Downs and passes Fovant Hut (002267).

The 'huts' on the ridgeways in this area originated as primitive establishments at which the villagers sold food and drink to travellers, a fact confirmed by Colt Hoare when he described Fovant Hut as having 'once proved a useful and comfortable *taberna* to the benighted traveller over these bleak and uninhabited heights'.

Chiselbury Camp

Soon after passing Fovant Hut the Salisbury Way crosses the road from Fovant to Fifield Bavant and after a further half mile passes a little wood on the left through which a beautiful hollow way followed by a public footpath joins the the ridgeway after slanting up Fovant Down from near Fovant Quarry. Chiselbury Camp, the Iron Age hillfort overlooking Fovant, is then passed on the left. This circular fortress was probably constructed in about 200 BC. It encloses an area of about nine acres within ramparts which generally consist of a single

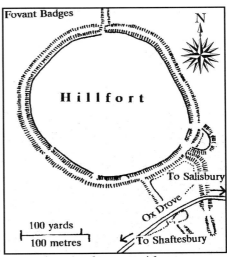

bank and ditch, although the ramparts on its south-west side are more substantial. Chiselbury provides outstanding views to the north over the villages of Compton Chamberlayne and Dinton to Great Ridge Wood.

On the downside below the hillfort are the Fovant chalk-cut badges, many of which which were created by soldiers during the First World War although they have subsequently been augmented by more badges. Being on the steep north-facing slope these badges are not visible from the Salisbury Way, but they are crossed by a footpath which runs north from the Salisbury Way round the east edge of the hillfort and down to East Farm at Fovant village.

The British and Colonial soldiers who created the Fovant hillside badges during the Great War were accommodated in the many camps created in the Nadder Valley on either side of the A30 around Swallowcliffe and Fovant. Fovant Camp stood principally east of the lane (007294) east of Fovant that runs north from the A30 to Fovant Wood, although some of the camp extended south of the A30. The rifle ranges were also south of the road, the firing being into the north flank of Fovant Down. The camp was served by a military railway that ran south from Dinton Station, across the Nadder, and immediately east of Fovant village. Other First World War camps were north of the A30 east of Compton Chamberlayne, and Hurdcott Camp south of the main road opposite the west end of Burcombe Ivers.

Wilton and its Literary Associations

Wilton House, standing in its park a mile and a half north of the Salisbury Way, opposite the Hare Warren, became a kind of academy of literature at the time of Henry, the 2nd Earl of Pembroke from 1570-1601, and William, the 3rd Earl from 1601-1630. Mary, Countess of Pembroke (1561-1621), wife of the second earl, was both learned and beautiful. She spent much of her time on literary studies with her brother Sir Philip Sidney who dedicated his *Arcadia* to her.

After Sidney was killed in 1586 she devoted her life to literature and became a generous patron to many men of letters. Her dedication to literature may have led to trouble in her marriage because when her husband Henry, the 2nd Earl of Pembroke (1534-1601) died he deliberately left her poorly provided for. James I was generous to her and gave her Ampthill Park in Bedfordshire. Her son William, 3rd Earl of Pembroke (1580-1630), inherited the literary tastes of his mother and uncle and continued the literary patronage that she had provided from Wilton. His son Philip, the 4th Earl (1584-1650), was named after Sir Philip Sidney. During the Civil War he sided with Parliament.

Mary, Dowager Countess of Pembroke's, beautiful epitaph was written by William Browne (1590?-1645?) – not Ben Jonson as has sometimes been alleged:

> *Underneath this sable hearse*
> *Lies the subject of all verse:*
> *Sidney's sister, Pembroke's mother:*
> *Death, ere though hast slain another*
> *Fair, and learned, and good as she,*
> *Time shall throw a dart at thee.*

John Aubrey tells us that 'In her time Wilton was like a college, there were so many learned and ingenious persons'. The galaxy of brilliant literary figures who were frequently at Wilton included Edmund Spenser (c.1552-1599), Sir Philip Sidney (1554-1586), Samuel Daniel (1562-1619), William Shakespeare (1564-1616), Ben Jonson (c.1573-1637), and later Isaak Walton (1593-1640) and George Herbert (1593-1633), who was related to the Pembrokes. The playwright Philip Massinger (1583-1640) was the son of a family retainer of the Pembrokes at Wilton.

In more recent times the once popular poet Sir Henry Newbolt (1862-

1938) – the writer of 'Drake's Drum' and other patriotic poetry – lived at Netherhampton House a little north of Salisbury Racecourse. The writer and broadcaster A.G. Street (1892-1966), the author of *The Gentleman of the Party* (1936) describing farming and the impact of the Great War on the Nadder Valley, lived at Ditchampton Farm near Wilton where his daughter, the writer Pamela Street, was brought up.

Another writer, Edith Olivier (1873-1948), lived in The Daye House at the east end of Wilton Park and there entertained many figures prominent in the arts prior to the Second World War. These included Siegfried Sassoon, Rex and Laurence Whistler, Cecil Beaton, the Sitwells, and the composer Sir William Walton. It was at Wilton that Walton composed part of his only symphony in March 1932. Another composer, Sir Hubert Parry (1848-1919), married a Pembroke and was frequently at Wilton House where in 1887 he composed 'Blest Pair of Sirens'.

Wilton House; south front added in the 1660s.

109

In this area occasional army huts may still be seen which survive from that time. The building of these camps provided the subject for A.G. Street's *The Gentleman of the Party*, a novel which very successfully describes farming life in the Nadder Valley from 1872, evoking the disruptive times of the camp building at the start of the war in 1914, and the reversion back to normality after the war.

Opposite Chiselbury there was a toll-gate on the ridgeway when it was a turnpike road, and a little farther east was another hut, Compton Hut (046287), which was situated on the south side of the Salisbury Way at the head of Hut Bottom but is now gone without trace.

North of Chiselbury and only a mile from the Salisbury Way is Compton Chamberlayne, a village which will be found to be as attractive as its name. Here is a beautiful grouping of a fine church, a lake and the manor house which was the seat of the Penruddocke family. In 1655 Colonel John Penruddocke (1619-55) led a desperate rebellion against the Commonwealth in an attempt to place Charles II on the throne. His revolt was in part prompted by the fact that he had become indebted as a result of Compton Park being seized by Parliament because both he and his father had fought for the king. Cromwell admired Colonel Penruddocke but reluctantly agreed to his execution and he was beheaded at Exeter. It was the Penruddocke rising that persuaded Cromwell to divide the entire country into military districts, each placed in the iron grip of a major-general, in an attempt to stifle any future rebellions against the Commonwealth.

Along the steep escarpment north of the Salisbury Way the unusual place-name 'Ivers' – the word is from the Old English *yfers* meaning steep slope or escarpment' – recurs in the names Sutton Ivers, Compton Ivers and Burcombe Ivers above the villages of those names ('Ivers' also occurs in West Ivers Wood and East Ivers Wood immediately east of Winkelbury Hill north of the Ox Drove).

The Salisbury Way continues eastwards to pass the Hare Warren above Wilton and Salisbury racecourse, where it crosses (at 104282) the Roman road from Old Sarum to Badbury Rings before descending into Salisbury. Over this stretch of the way from Chiselbury to the Hare Warren the Salisbury Way is sometimes lined by high hedges through which only intermittent glimpses are obtained of the wide views to Grovely Wood to the north and to the ridge followed by the Ox Drove to the south. As it passes the Hare Warren woods the Salisbury Way loses most of its downland character and becomes a tree-shaded way until it reaches Salisbury Racecourse and descends a track which is roughly metalled with stone to Harnham Hill and Salisbury.

The Ox Drove Ridgeway

The southern of the two ridgeways which follow the chalk downland watersheds across the south of Wiltshire is the Ox Drove which runs along the ridge between the River Ebble and the woods of Cranborne Chase which straddle the Wiltshire-Dorset boundary. The Ox Drove commences near Win Green Hill on the Dorset border two miles north of Ashmore where several tributary droveways combine to become the single ridgeway which runs for ten miles along the ridge south of the River Ebble, gently declining in height to a point south of Bishopstone where for three quarters of a mile it joins the A354 before diverging from the road to cross Grim's Ditch to possibly continue east through Downton.

The Ox Drove running east from Win Green.

Unlike the roughly parallel Salisbury Way on the Ebble-Nadder ridge to its north, the Ox Drove was never turnpiked and always remained a secondary route which made it attractive to drovers who liked to follow unfrequented routes with their flocks and herds. Its name commemorates the fact that this south Wiltshire ridgeway was used as a toll-free highway by droves of cattle moving east towards London out of Somerset and Dorset at a time when all beef was walked on-the-hoof to the metropolis. The Ox Drove finally lost any importance it had when the valley road along the Ebble Valley was opened in 1758 and left the ridgeway entirely to the drovers.

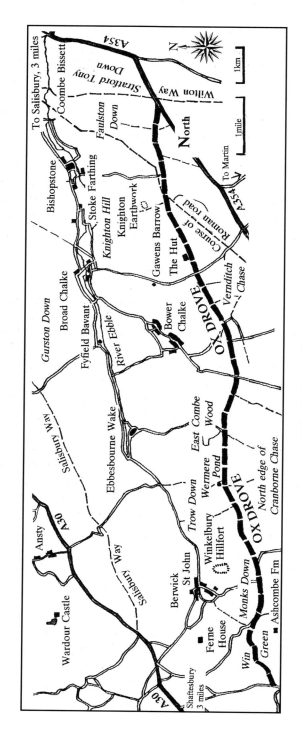

The Ox Drove Ridgeway

Droving along the Ox Drove

The droving trade flourished from the time late in the Middle Ages when the rapidly expanding larger towns became too large to subsist off the produce of their immediate surroundings, until the mid-19th century when the trade was effectively terminated by the advent of the railways and their cattle trucks. Throughout this period large droves, mainly of cattle (but also of sheep, pigs, horses and sometimes poultry), followed the network of droveways which had adopted green ways upon which no tolls were levied, which were gentle to the feet of the animals, and provided free grazing along the way. These droveways became a recognised secondary and alternative system of roads to the turnpike system. Just as the Salisbury Way was defined by the Earl of Pembroke with lime trees at mile intervals, the Ox Drove is irregularly marked by Scots pines which are known to have been planted as markers for droveways.

The Ox Drove commences at a height of 909 feet (277 m) near Win Green Hill in the extreme south-west of Wiltshire. From Win Green panoramic views may be enjoyed, over Shaftesbury to the west, to the ridge followed by the Salisbury Way ridgeway to the north, and on a clear day to the Isle of Wight thirty miles away to the south-east. After leaving Win Green the Ox Drove runs for several miles immediately north of Cranborne Chase. At the west end of Monk's Down the ground plunges away from the Ox Drove on both sides, to the north towards Ferne House (930223) and Berwick St John, and to the south into Ashcombe. Despite its name Monk's Down has no monastic connection. It derives its name from the Monk family who owned a small clock factory in Berwick St John which operated from 1550 to 1800, making violins as well as church and domestic clocks.

Ferne House is associated with the poet Shelley (1792-1822) who, at the age of seventeen, was engaged to his beautiful cousin Harriet Grove, a daughter of the Groves of Ferne House. She was a writer in her own right and some chapters of *Zastrozzi*, published by Shelley when he was at Eton, are believed to be by her. Harriet became alarmed at Shelley's republican politics and anti-clericism and broke off the engagement. In 1811 Shelley was expelled from Oxford for alleged atheism and eloped with the sixteen year old girl Harriet Westbrook whom he ultimately married. Harriet Grove married William Hellyar of nearby Sedgehill, the heir to Coker Court near Yeovil, and by doing so provoked the outcry from Shelley: 'She is gone! she is lost to me for ever! She married! Married to a clod of earth'.

It is also of interest to note another association of this area with a Victorian poet. Robert Browning's (1812-89) paternal great grandfather owned the inn at Woodyates two miles south of the Ox Drove and just over the Dorset boundary.

South from Monk's Down are long views into Dorset past the former Romano-British villages at Berwick Down (942196) and Rotherley Down (949196) which were excavated by General Pitt-Rivers who on Rotherley Down set up a stone obelisk upon which he recorded the average stature of the male and female skeletons found here. Despite its modest size this obelisk is just visible from the Ox Drove. A similar Romano-British village at Woodcutts (963182), just over the county boundary in Dorset, was also excavated by Pitt-Rivers and is well worth visiting for at Woodcutts the earthworks are more elaborate and better preserved.

Rushmore House and Park

General Pitt-Rivers lived at Rushmore House in the large Georgian mansion built one and a half miles south of the Ox Drove on the site of the former Rushmore Lodge. Rushmore had a long history as the principal hunting lodge for Cranborne Chase. Around it was created a small deer park by Robert Cecil (c.1563-1612), the first Earl of Salisbury and principal adviser to James I, who was granted the rights to the Chase and the ownership of Rushmore early in the 17th century. The estate later passed to the Earls of Shaftesbury, and through them to the Rivers family and ultimately to General Pitt-Rivers. Subsequently Rushmore House became Sandroyd School.

Immediately west of Rushmore House lies the beautiful secluded coombe of Tinkley Bottom (949184) along which runs a public footpath from Tollard Royal to Berwick and Rotherley Downs and ultimately to the Ox Drove. Here I once saw, within the space of a few minutes one fine October afternoon, a fallow deer buck, a barn owl hunting, two soaring buzzards and several green woodpeckers, a memorable experience that I do not suppose I shall ever repeat.

Cranborne Chase

In the area south of the Ox Drove many woodland walks are available in the extensive woods of Cranborne Chase, an ancient hunting ground and former haunt of smugglers described by Thomas Hardy as 'a truly venerable tract of forest land, one of the few remaining woodlands in England of truly primeval date'. Cranborne was a private Chase rather than a Royal Forest, belonging to the Duke of Gloucester although it passed to King John when he married the Duke's daughter Isabella. Its northern boundary was once as far north as the River Nadder, but in common with most medieval hunting grounds it has now been greatly reduced in area. The hunting rights of Cranborne Chase were finally extinguished by an Act of Parliament of 1828 which disenfranchised The Chase. By this time violent pitched battles between the keepers, who were defending the ancient rights of the Chase and gentlemen-poachers, who resented and challenged them, were not unusual. In one affray in 1791 ten keepers engaged ten poachers near Rushmore.

The Ox Drove (continued)

From Monk's Down to a point opposite the splendid Iron Age fort of Winkelbury (952217), which thrusts its massive promontory north to loom over Berwick St John, the Ox Drove is metalled for almost a mile before again becoming a green way. Over most of this metalled stretch the only views are to the north over the valley of the River Ebble, the views to the south being here blocked by a belt of trees, although they open up again near Winkelbury.

It was on the Ox Drove opposite Winkelbury that many years ago I first heard sheep bells, having chanced upon a flock with its senior ewe wearing a bell. Sheep wearing bells are of course unusual these days, and I was so intrigued that I caught the ewe to examine its bell. Subsequently I have heard sheep bells on a number of occasions, more frequently in south Wiltshire than in the north of the county.

The impressively sited hillfort of Winkelbury encloses about twelve acres. Excavation by Pitt Rivers in 1881-2 revealed occupation through the Iron Age, and an Anglo-Saxon cemetery at the point where the promontory joins the down. Local traditions about this ceme-tery may explain the fact that until compara-tively recent times a dead tree known as the 'Winkelbury Scragg' was carefully maintained at the highest point of Winkelbury in the belief that its existence served as a charm against witches and evil spirits.

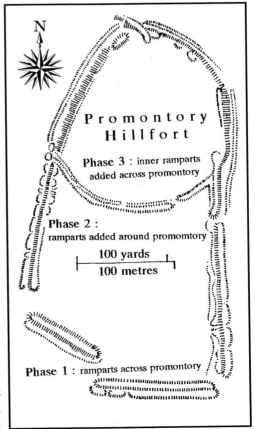

N

Promontory Hillfort

Phase 3 : inner ramparts added across promontory

Phase 2 : ramparts added around promomtory

100 yards

100 metres

Phase 1 : ramparts across promontory

General Pitt-Rivers and Archaeology

General Pitt-Rivers (1827-1900) was born A.H.Lane Fox, became a soldier and pursued a military career, but developed a passion for archaeology. He retired from the service as a result of poor health and became Vice President of the Society of Antiquaries. He was a very distant relative of the 2nd Baron Rivers with many relatives between him and the inheritance, but in 1880 he unexpectedly inherited the vast Cranborne Chase Estate, partly in Wiltshire but principally in Dorset. As a condition of his inheritance he adopted the surname Pitt-Rivers and  for the rest of his life devoted his great organisational ability and his newly acquired fortune to archaeological excavation, becoming a pioneer of modern methods of archaeology.

Pitt-Rivers was a dedicated man who regarded social activity as frivolous. On one occasion his wife was mystified by the failure of any guests to arrive at one of her social functions. She was entirely unaware that the general had arranged for all the gates of Rushmore to be locked!

General Pitt-Rivers felt an obligation to share his good fortune and created the Larmer Tree Pleasure Grounds (941169), south of Tollard Royal, to which the public were admitted free of charge. These grounds take their name from the Larmer Tree under which King John is said to have met his huntsmen when he was at his Tollard Royal estate which he inherited from his wife. Having long been completely private the Larmer Tree Grounds are now regularly open for the public to see the exotic Indian and Classical buildings which formed the backdrop to the band concerts and performances which General Pitt-Rivers presented for the public from the 1880s to his death in 1900. These grounds became extremely popular and at the peak of their popularity in 1899 no less than 44,417 people visited performances here, although at General Pitt-River's death in 1900 all public functions at the grounds ceased.

North of the Larmer Tree Grounds a footpath passes through the Tollard Park Arabian Stud. From personal experience I would recommend avoiding walking this right of way among the excitable and highly-strung stallions.

At the end of Bridmore Belt a little beyond Winkelbury the Ox Drove is joined from the north (at 954207) by a hollow-way which has run up the east flank of Winkelbury Hill from the valley near Berwick St John. After the conclusive defeat of his peasant army at the Battle of Sedgemoor on 5-6 July 1685 in his attempt to wrest the throne from James II, the Duke of Monmouth in his flight south-eastwards passed through Berwick St John on his way to Woodyates where he exchanged clothes with a local peasant. He is believed to have followed this hollow-way up the east flank of Winkelbury, in which case he would have followed the Ox Drove east from here to above Bower Chalke before turning south to Woodyates. On this stretch of the Ox Drove I often conjure up an image of the forlorn Duke, his high hopes dashed and his cause irrevocably lost, attempting with his companions to evade James I's troopers and escape to the Continent. He failed and was caught hiding in a ditch near Horton in Dorset, was taken to London and – being the subject of a Bill of Attainder – was executed without trial within a week.

Win Green from Winkelbury Hill

H.J. Massingham evoked the ancient history of the Ox Drove near Winkelbury and this Monmouth incident in *English Downland* (1935):

Where I stand is full of history. Behind me the camp [Winkelbury], constructed like Chiselbury, follows the elongated contour of the hill.

117

There the cattle in a raid were herded up the sunken ways from the springs below and, on the other or southern side of the cross-rampart, dwelt the first Celts of the Iron Age; hardy on their buffetted height, men of little substance, reckoning nothing of the movements of history in their eyrie and fearing only the rustlers from the greater strongholds of Hambledon, Badbury, or Whitsbury. Monmouth fled along this Ox Drove after Sedgemoor, the Romans modernised it on their way to Mendip, but the megalith-builders, by their barrows beside it, were its pioneers.

Soon after passing the isolated and derelict Bigley Buildings (976216) on South Down above Alvediston, the way passes immediately south of Wermere Pond (976217), now a much reduced ancient embanked pond on Elcombe Down but formerly one of the boundary marks of Cranborne Chase. Between East Combe Wood and near Middle Chase Farm the Ox Drove is again under tarmacadam for a mile over Woodminton Down before reverting to being a green way.

At Cow Down Hill south of Bower Chalke the Ox Drove crosses the minor road from Misselfore to Woodyates and passes within a few hundred yards of the Dorset boundary. The road intersection known as Kit's Grave (025214), a little south of the Ox Drove on the Wiltshire-Dorset boundary, is said to be haunted by the ghost of a poor girl who committed suicide and was buried here in unconsecrated ground. The Saxon charters name the point *Cheoteles heafde* and beside it on the Dorset side of the county boundary is Chettles Head Copse.

Vernditch Chase

After passing Marleycombe Hill (023223) above Bower Chalke the Ox Drove skirts the north edge of Vernditch Chase, a delightful wood of oak standards, hazel coppice and beech between Bower Chalke and the Dorset boundary. This wood, together with Stonedown Wood (994203) which was passed earlier, was formerly known as Gardiner Forest from being owned by the composer Balfour Gardiner (1877-1950) who with the assistance of his forester nephew Rolf Gardiner (1902-1971) embarked on extensive tree-planting on the Gardiner estates in Cranborne Chase. Rolf Gardiner, whose son is the distinguished conductor John Eliot Gardiner, expressed the philosophy of their forestry activities in Cranborne Chase in an article headed 'A Farm in Cranborne Chase' in *The Countryman* (Vol.70, No.1, Spring 1978):

During a period of more than forty years, first [my uncle] Balfour

John Aubrey at Broad Chalke

The Wiltshire antiquary and gossip John Aubrey (1626-1697) lived for a time at a farm at Broad Chalke. He loved this part of Wiltshire, and hoped that he might be buried beside Gawen's Barrow (036235), the now-flattened tumulus under a mile north of the Ox Drove on Knowle Hill beside the road from Martin to Broad Chalke which offers such fine views west over Bower Chalke. Aubrey wrote: 'I never was so sacralegious as to disturbe, or rob his urne but I have oftentimes wish't that my  Corps might be interred by it,' but he was buried at Oxford. Aubrey's many writings, well known to Wiltshire historians, are contained in *The Natural History of Wiltshire,* edited by John Britton in 1847, and in other papers that were edited by Canon Jackson in 1862 as *Wiltshire: the Topographical Collections of John Aubrey*. He is best known for his *Brief Lives*, an invaluable series of short biographies of his friends and contemporaries.

Maurice Hewlett

At the Old Rectory at Broad Chalke – said to have originally been the residence of the Prebendaries of Chalke who were wealthy ecclesiastics under the Plantagenet kings – lived for many years the novelist, essayist and poet Maurice Hewlett (1861-1923) who enjoyed a great success, which he regarded as excessive, with his first book *The Forest Lovers* (1898), a romantic novel set in the Middle Ages. Hewlett regarded himself as primarily a poet. His great work was 'The Song of the Plow' (1916), a long-neglected poem which describes the history of the English farm worker from Norman times. In 1921 he published *Wiltshire Essays*. Hewlett loved this part of Wiltshire and was a great advocate of its attractions. Among his visitors to Broad Chalke was Ezra Pound (1885-1972), the American-born Imagist (anti-Romantic) poet.

Maurice Hewlett's grave is on private ground on a local farm. He is commemorated by a brass on the inside south wall of the church.

Christopher Wood

Opposite the Old Rectory at Broade Chalke stands Reddish House, a fine early-18th century Baroque house which was the home of the family of Christopher Wood (1901-1930), the promising young painter whose father was the local doctor. After a protracted illness had forced him to leave Marlborough College, Christopher Wood discovered whilst convalescing an unexpected talent for painting. He decided to become a painter and in 1921 went to Paris where he associated with Cocteau, Diaghilev, and Picasso. He was also a friend of Ben Nicholson. His health was never good, he took to drugs, and enjoyed only limited success.

His first major show coincided with the Wall Street crash, and he spent the last two summers of his life painting at Treboul on the coast of Brittany. In 1930 Christopher Wood took his life by throwing himself under a train at Salisbury station. He is buried in Broad Chalke churchyard where his grave slab, beautifully lettered by Eric Gill, may be seen near the south porch of the church. After the Wood family left Reddish House it was taken by Sir Cecil Beaton (1904-1980) after his lease at Ashcombe had run out and was not renewed. He is also buried in Broad Chalke churchyard.

[Gardiner], at my instigation, and then I alone planted some three million trees on the chalk downs and among the hazel coppices of this impoverished north-west district of Cranborne Chase. We altered the whole appearance and configuration of the landscape. In the 'twenties the hills were almost entirely bare, badly eroded with rabbit scrapes and screes, with surreptitious downwash leaching the topsoil over the chalk, a process uninterrupted since the time of the prehistoric settlers. I was determined to restore in some measure the hill-and-vale economy devised by the Saxon minsters which created the manors and parishes of Wessex.

Vernditch Chase was formerly a great deal larger than it is today. As late as 1773 Andrews and Dury showed it as extending from its present position to several miles farther north-east with its eastern limits at Faulston Down in the north and near Toyd Farm in the south. Vernditch Lodge was situated at the south-west end of Knighton Wood where Old Lodge Coppice is shown on modern maps.

This Chase – a 'Chase' or 'Chace' was a hunting ground owned by a subject rather than the king – had been in the estate of the Earl of Pembroke, and Aubrey tells us that this wood was to a great extent the inspiration for Sir Philip Sidney's *Arcadia* (1580), a book that was essentially a romance containing a diversity of romantic episodes with passages of exquisite beauty set in the imaginary country of Arcadia, the name which originated as an idyllic part of Greece. The book had a terrific vogue and was read by Charles I on the scaffold at Whitehall. Aubrey writes:

> But the Arcadia and Daphne is about Vernditch and Wilton; and these romancy plaines and boscages did no doubt conduce to the heightening of Sir Philip Sydney's phansie. He lived much in these parts [at Wilton House where his sister was the wife of the Earl of Pembroke], and his most masterly touches of his pastoralls he wrote here upon the spott, where they were conceived. 'Twas about these purlieus that the muses were wont to appear to Sir Philip Sydney, and where he wrote down their dictates in his table book, though on horseback.

Early in the 18th century, at the time of the savage affrays between keepers and deer-poachers in Cranborne Chase, one of Lord Pembroke's keepers was beaten to death in Vernditch. Only one of his assailants was caught, and he was hanged in chains in Vernditch at the site of his crime.

Vernditch is an extremely beautiful wood and when an old Wiltshire shepherd was asked to explain his idea of heaven he suggested that it would probably resemble Vernditch Chase but with the addition of a stream down its middle. This wood is a glorious place to walk, especially in spring when the beech foliage is translucent and the wood is carpeted with bluebells. Access is good, with footpaths along its south-west edge, which coincides with the Dorset boundary, and another along the Roman road which has a pronounced agger resembling a railway embankment as it follows the county boundary along the south-east edge of Vernditch. Chickengrove Bottom on the north side of Vernditch has now been designated a nature reserve.

After leaving Vernditch Chase the Ox Drove crosses a minor road on Knowle Hill. To the north the road passes through a delightful beech avenue to Broad Chalke, to the south along the edge of Vernditch to Martin Drove End and Martin. From this crossing the wooded Badbury Rings can be seen through the gap to the south thirteen miles away in Dorset.

Vernditch Chase, the Gardiner Forest beside the Ox Drove, seen from the Roman Road which follows its south-east edge.

A few hundred yards after crossing this road the Ox Drove passes The Hut and Lodge Farm. The 'Hut' names of south Wiltshire were, as already noted in connection with Fovant Hut on the Salisbury Way, establishments at which food and drink were provided for drovers and travellers. In his *Anecdotes of Cranborne Chase* (1818) William Chafin relates that in the 18th century The Hut was a public house where a musical club led by a Mr Henry Goode of Broad Chalke met regularly to perform, and incidentally poach the deer of the Chase! Andrews and Dury in 1773 showed The Hut as 'Inoculation House'.

North of the Ox Drove opposite The Hut the countryside between Broad Chalke and The Hut offers fine walking in an area that is of such quality that several nature reserves have recently been opened in this district, including a large one on Middleton Down west of Church Bottom with its entrance at 046238.

For three miles from The Hut to New Farm the Ox Drove runs parallel to Grim's Ditch, an ancient linear earthwork that still coincides with the Wiltshire-

Dorset boundary from the south-west corner of Knighton Wood through Swayne's Firs on the A354 to Toyd Clump (090229) on Little Toyd Down.

After passing the head of Church Bottom – the delightful secluded coombe which is followed by an inviting footpath which runs down to Broad Chalke – the Ox Drove crosses near Knighton Wood (at 062232) the Roman road from Badbury Rings to Old Sarum. The Roman *agger* can be seen running south-west and following the north-west edge of Knighton Wood and the south-east edge of Vernditch Chase. As indicated earlier, Knighton Wood was formerly part of the then much more extensive Vernditch Chase.

Church Bottom running from the Ox Drove down to Broad Chalke.

Six hundred yards north of the Ox Drove is Knighton Earthworks (058239), the prehistoric Iron Age and Romano-British settlement named by the Anglo-Saxons *Wudu burh* meaning 'camp of the wood'. East of Knighton Wood the Ox Drove becomes a minor and very little-used lane. On Faulston Down it passes (at 081234) the head of Faulston Drove in which, according to John Aubrey who lived for a time at nearby Broad Chalke, the boy King Edward VI was lost by his courtiers when hunting.

Here the Ox Drove widens in a broad stony lane and near New Farm it joins the A354 main road and is crossed by the Wilton Way (the *Wilton Weie* of the Anglo-Saxons) which follows a direct northerly route out of west Hampshire to cross the Ebble at the Roman ford at Stratford (*Streat ford*) Tony.

The Wilton Way

Fish from the Dorset ports was carried along Wilton Way by packhorse to markets at Devizes and Salisbury. During the Middle Ages the Church nominated certain days when meat eating was forbidden. For these days fish was in demand as a substitute for the forbidden meat, and fish became even more important during the reign of Elizabeth I when an Act was passed enforcing both Fridays and Saturdays as 'fish days' when fish must be eaten, the purpose of the Act being to encourage the fisheries which trained the sailors needed by the Navy. The Wilton Way would then have gained in importance as a trade route. It must later have been followed by smugglers carrying their contraband cargoes inland from the south coast.

Today the Wilton Way provides good walking south from the Ox Drove where there is excellent walking in the neighbourhood of Martin and Damerham, particularly in the area of Martin Down and Bokerly Dyke south-west from Martin which now marks the boundary between Dorset and Hampshire. The village of Martin, two miles east of Vernditch and now in Hampshire, was the fictional 'Winterbourne Bishop' of W.H.Hudson's Wiltshire classic *A Shepherd's Life*, subtitled 'Impressions of the South Wiltshire Downs'. Prior to boundary changes in 1895 Martin was in Wiltshire, but by the time *A Shepherd's Life* was published in 1910 it had been transferred to Hampshire, a fact which put the journalists right off the scent when they were scouring south Wiltshire trying to establish the location of Hudson's 'Winterbourne Bishop'. The Martin district is so very remote that it was described by H. Moutray Read in *Highways and Byways in Hampshire* (1908) as being at 'the end of all things where Martin lies'. Near here, at Rushay Farm in Pentridge, was born the Dorset dialect poet William Barnes (1801-86) who for a time kept school at the Old Chantry House beside Mere church in Wiltshire.

Damerham has a little-known Civil War association in that Denzil Holles (1599-1680), who was one of the five members whom Charles I had tried to arrest in Parliament and by his attempt finally precipitated the Civil War, lived at Damerham during the early part of the war, having married the daughter of Sir Francis Ashley of Dorchester who bequeathed Damerham to him. Holles fell out of sympathy with Cromwell because of his Parliamentary principles and was widely believed to have been involved in the Clubmen movement (already mentioned in Chapter 10) which attempted to force a peace on both the opposing sides. He had been an active soldier early in the Civil War, but during the winter of 1642-3 he had advocated peace and thus became suspect to both Parliament and its army. With Sir Philip Stapleton, Holles led the moderate Presbyterian party in Parliament which in 1647 devised a programme that might have secured a compromise settlement with the king, but the army marched on London and purged Parliament of its more moderate 'eleven members'. Holles was in some danger from the war party, and in January 1648 he was impeached by the army, but survived and ultimately came to terms with Charles II.

The Ox Drove (cont.)

Towards its eastern end, a little after leaving the A354 beyond New Farm, the Ox Drove becomes less definite and no longer a ridgeway. From a height of 536 feet (163m) near The Hut it remains high (521 feet or 159m) near New Farm, but over the next mile and a half it descends as it crosses Grim's Ditch and for half a mile enters Dorset before at Great Yews re-entering Wiltshire at a height of 377 feet (115m). It then probably runs on east-south-east and at Gallows Hill on Wick Down turns due east to cross the Salisbury Avon at Downton.

Yew woods are particularly rare in Wiltshire, and isolated yew trees are unusual except for those deliberately planted in churchyards. Great Yews adjoins Hampshire where yew trees are more common, so much so that they became known as the 'Hampshire weed'.

Throughout its length from New Farm to Downton the Ox Drove remains a public right of way, but it is no longer recognisable as the glorious Ox Drove ridgeway which we have followed across south Wiltshire from Win Green to south of Coombe Bissett, and indeed this stretch from New Farm to Downton is questionable. Salisbury was a great centre for the droving trade with great fairs and markets. Consequently much of the Ox Drove traffic from New Farm would have turned north-east through Coombe Bissett along the line of the present A354 and joined the Salisbury Way in its descent of Harnham Hill to Salisbury and its markets.

The Area between the Salisbury Way and the Ox Drove

The area between the two roughly parallel south Wiltshire ridgeways must now be described. At their western ends the Salisbury Way at White Sheet and the Ox Drove on Monks Down are merely two miles apart. They then diverge to be about three miles apart opposite Broad Chalke, and narrow again as they near Salisbury so that there is only two miles between them opposite Coombe Bissett. Within this area between the two ridgeways there is much excellent walking on both sides of the River Ebble, which being sometimes known as the Chalke gave its name to the villages of Bower Chalke and Broad Chalke.

The succession of attractive and delightfully named villages and hamlets

– Berwick St John, Alvediston, the intriguing Ebbesbourne Wake which derives its name from Ebble Bourne, Fifield Bavant, Broad Chalke, Stoke Farthing, Bishopstone, Stratford Tony and Coombe Bissett – are all well worth visiting and can be incorporated in walks from the ridges across the valley.

Norrington Manor near Alvediston

In the countryside between the Salisbury Way and the Ox Drove towards their west ends stands Norrington Manor House. Domestic architecture of the 14th century is rare in Wiltshire and here at Norrington we have one of the most complete examples, exquisitely situated in the downs a little west of Alvediston (966238). The house belonged to the ancient family of Gawens. John Aubrey, writing in the late 17th century, tells us that 'the Gawens had long been settled in this place', and that 'they had resided here 450 and odd years, until it was disposed of to Sir William Wyndham (in 1658)'. They may have been the family of Sir Gawaine, a hero of the early Arthurian legends who in Malory's *Morte d'Arthur* was the son of King Arthur's sister and had many adventures in search of the Holy Grail. Sir Gawaine became the enemy of Sir Lancelot and was wounded and died at Dover when King Arthur landed to recover his kingdom from his nephew Mordred.

Norrington Manor west of Alvediston.

Norrington Manor has a hall, porch, and undercroft, all begun in 1377 at the start of the reign of Richard II. The hall has two-light windows with Perpendicular tracery, and the porch has a particularly fine moulded arch. The solar wing was rebuilt in the 17th century over the original vaulted undercroft. Norrington Manor may be viewed from the public footpath which runs past its south front. It is reached by a footpath which leaves the Salisbury Way at 962248, or by a green way which runs north from Trow Down on the Ox Drove (at 970213) and skirts Windmill Hill.

When the prolonged continuation of Forest Law over Cranborne Chase had become oppressive in the early 19th century Mr King of Norrington, situated on the edge of the Chase, challenged Lord Rivers over his forest rights. The case came to court in Salisbury in 1816 and Lord Rivers' rights were restricted, although he was able to establish his rights for 'running through' a large area of country. On the whole Mr King won his case, to the delight of the local people who had long suffered from Lord Rivers' high-handed behaviour and insistence on exerting the archaic rights of Cranborne Chase over so vast an area.

Gallows Hill, the 18th century execution hill, from north of Norrington Manor.

Three-quarters of a mile north-west of Norrington Manor is Gallows Hill (955243), the promontory of down extending from the ridge along which the Salisbury Way turnpike ran from White Sheet Hill to Salisbury. The original gallows was one of a group of Scots pines which existed in 1937, but are now gone. In his *Salisbury Plain* (1955) Ralph Whitlock recalled seeing the gallows tree in the mid-1950s. This Scots pine had a horizontal branch about eight feet from the ground pointing west and scarred by the chains of many executions. The trunk of the tree, which was visible from the turnpike, was notched to provide steps for the executioner. In 1927 many 18th century bottles were discovered buried under the tree, surviving from wakes held when executions were regarded as public spectacles. Although Gallows Hill is surrounded by public rights of way, none of them runs on to the hill.

Bishopstone

Bishopstone is an attractive dispersed village strung along the River Ebble, much of the village being a mile west of its church, with pretty scenery along the roads which cross the river. Its dispersed character probably arises from the fact that during the Black Death in 1349, when it has been estimated that from a third to half of England's population died, Bishopstone suffered so severely that scarcely a person survived and when the area was repopulated its new residents adopted new sites out of fear at their memories of the high mortality.

At Faulston to the east of Bishopstone the circular dovecot of banded flint and stone with a conical roof was formed out of a tower of the castle which belonged to William de Braose. He was a loyal supporter of King John who nonetheless decided that he had become too powerful, hounded him out of his vast estates and, according to the contemporary chroniclers, starved his wife Matilda and one of his sons to death in a dungeon. At Faulston the Parliamentary Committee that during the Civil War levied fines on 'malignants' – that is persons who adhered to the Royalist cause – used to meet. Bishopstone church, which stands a mile east of the village at Throope, is alleged to have bullet marks on the outside of its chancel wall from the time when Royalist prisoners were shot after the Penruddocke rising against Cromwell in 1655, although I must admit that I have never succeeded in finding them.

The Roman Road across the Ebble Valley

In its crossing of the Ebble Valley from Salisbury racecourse (104282) to near Knighton Wood (061232), after fording the river at Stratford Tony the Roman road from Old Sarum to Badbury Rings in Dorset executes an unusual side-step in three straight lengths to avoid the coombes which run south-east from the valley at Stoke Farthing. The Roman road over this diversion remains as a public right of way (from 080255 in Faulston Drove to 080248 where it leaves the droveway at a bend, runs from 070234 on the open downs to 061232, and on to the Ox Drove). This stepping of a Roman road out of its true line to avoid a natural feature is unusual and represents a less dramatic example than the great loop taken by the Roman road at Chute Causeway described in Chapter 7. This stretch of the former Roman road across the downs above Bishopstone may easily be incorporated in walks across the Ebble Valley between the two ridgeways, as may the many footpaths which cross the valley of the Ebble and provide varied walks in the countryside associated with these two fine south Wiltshire ridgeways, the Salisbury Way and the Ox Drove.

The Wilton Way, which has already been mentioned as providing the approach to the Martin area, crosses the Ox Drove west of New Farm (at 091235). North of the Ox Drove it runs on exactly due north through Stratford Tony and across the Roman road. After its river crossing the Wilton Way becomes a minor road in its rise from Stratford Tony to the Salisbury Way at the Hare Warren near the racecourse.

In recollecting my experiences in this area the one that comes immediately to mind is of walking one summer afternoon east from the quarry below White Sheet Hill the entire fifteen mile length of the Salisbury Way, past and around Chiselbury Camp, down into Salisbury and taking the bus back through the villages of the Nadder Valley to my starting point below White Sheet.

Bower Chalke from Marleycombe Hill.

Suggested Walks associated with the South Wiltshire Ridgeways

As is the case with the Ridgeway in north Wiltshire described in Chapter 1 of Volume 1, linear walks along the Salisbury Way and the Ox Drove ridgeway may obviously be followed in either direction, although they have been described west to east. The walks that are now suggested in the countryside closely associated with these south Wiltshire ridgeways are grouped as follows :-
  (a) north of the Salisbury Way to the Nadder Valley.
  (b) south of the Ox Drove towards Cranborne Chase.
  (c) between the Salisbury Way and the Ox Drove across the Ebble Valley.

(a) Walks north of the Salisbury Way

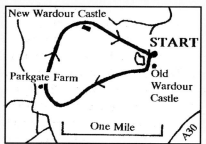

11A: The Wardour Area (3 miles: map 184):

The area of the Vale of Wardour north of the west end of the Salisbury Way may by explored by the following short 3 mile walk. After parking in the car park at Old Wardour Castle (938263) walk south past the castle and then west along the fenced track. This track crosses the site of the former Wardour Parks for red and fallow deer. At 932261 leave this track, continue south-westwards, and beyond Nower's Copse at 922254 turn north past Park Gate Farm to New Wardour Castle. The route from here back to Old Wardour Castle is south-east past Ark Farm. The Old Castle, which is in the care of the English Heritage, may be visited.

11B: Compton Chamberlayne
(diversion of 3 miles from the Ox Drove: map 184):
When walking the Salisbury Way the village of Compton Chamberlayne with its fine group of church, manor house and park may be visited by taking a short three mile circular walk from a point (036282) on the Salisbury Way at Compton Down. Compton Chamberlayne is reached by taking the western track down the hill (through Manor Farm) and across the A30. Be sure to visit the churchyard overlooking the lake and manor house before returning east from the village past Naishes Farm and then south across the A30 up the

track through 039289, regaining the Salisbury Way at the point from which it was left by an oblique climb up Compton Down. This walk may alternatively be followed as a walk in its own right (as opposed to a diversion from the Salisbury Way) by parking in the lay-by (027305) beside the lake a little north of Compton Chamberlayne.

(b) Walks south of the Ox Drove

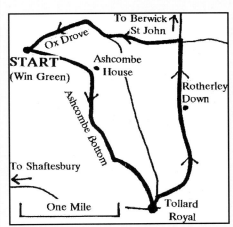

11C: Ashcombe and Tollard Royal from Win Green (6 miles: map 184): Cecil Beaton's former secluded house at Ashcombe may be seen by walking the public footpath which runs east from Win Green Hill (where there is a large hilltop car park) down the steep slope through woods into Ashcombe. Beaton loved Ashcombe and described his stay in *Ashcombe, the Story of a Fifteen-Year Lease* (1949). Near the house turn south and follow Ashcombe Bottom south and south-east to Tollard Royal. From Tollard Royal the return route to the Ox Drove is north-east along Tinkley Bottom (949184), the delightful park-like coombe between Tollard Royal and Rushmore Park. The continuation is north by the footpath over Rotherley Down with its Romano-British settlement to the Ox Drove. On Rotherley Down ensure that you avoid the track which swings to the right (north-east) around the head of Rotherley Bottom towards Higher Bridmore Farm. This unnecessarily extends the walk. The shorter route is along the unhedged way that runs true north across the fields towards the gap in the tree belt at 948206. From this point the return is west along 2 miles of the Ox Drove over Monk's Down back to Win Green.

11D: Monk's Down to Tollard Royal (5 miles: map 184):
The small car park at Monk's Down (937207) on the Ox Drove above Ashcombe may be used as the starting point for a similar fine walk south past the Romano-British settlement over Berwick Down to Tollard Royal, returning north west of Rushmore House along the route described in the previous walk past the Rotherley Down settlement to point 948206 on the Ox Drove three-quarters of a mile east of the starting point.

11E: Cranborne Chase from the Ox Drove (6 to 7 miles: map 184):

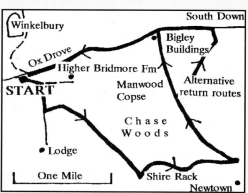

The sylvan delights of Cranborne Chase may be explored by parking beside the Ox Drove opposite Winkelbury (at 953207) and walking east and south down the tarmacadamed drive to 957201, then south-east through Chase Woods to Shire Rack (973190) on the county boundary – a name which probably derives from a 'shire oak' marking the shire boundary. Continue east along Shire Rack to north of Newton and there turn north-west and recross the Chase Woods to point 979202 east of Manwood Copse. From here the Ox Drove may be regained by alternative ways, one up the shoulder of down running north to Bigley Buildings (975216), the other north-east up the coombe to the west of Chase Barn to the Ox Drove on South Down (985216). My own preference is for the latter option. The return is then west along the Ox Drove.

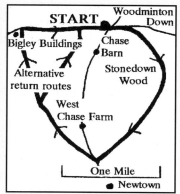

11F: Ox Drove to Stonedown Wood (4 miles: map 184):
Another approach to Cranborne Chase is south from a point (993216) near Chase Barn on a metalled section of the Ox Drove where a car may be parked. The walk is initially south-east then south down the footpath which follows the east edge of Stonedown Wood, part of Cranborne Chase. The return is from the county boundary north of Newtown along the alternative routes to the Ox Drove described

in Walk 11E above, past Manwood Copse and then east along the Ox Drove over South Down.

11G : Verndtich Chase from the Ox Drove (5 miles: map 184):

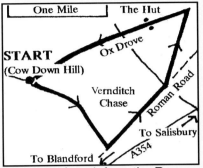

Cow Down Hill (023216) on the Ox Drove is a convenient place to park and then undertake a walk to Verndtich Chase, a wood which has a particularly rich flora. The walk is south-east down the county boundary, through Verndtich Chase to the Roman road at its southern edge. The prominent agger of the Roman road is then followed north-east to the minor road at 046215 where the path which diverges a little east of north from the Roman road is taken to reach the Ox Drove east of The Hut and Lodge Farm. The Ox Drove is then followed for two miles south-west back to Cow Down Hill.

(c) Walks between the Salisbury Way and the Ox Drove

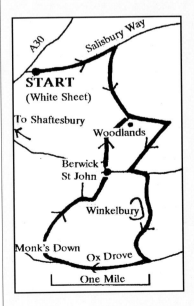

Problems over return transport often arise in connection with linear walks and walkers may prefer, as alternatives to linear walks along the ridges, to combine sections of the Salisbury Way and the Ox Drove into circular walks by walking across the Ebble Valley. As with most ridgeways the walks across the ridges into the surrounding countryside frequently offer more variety and are sometimes far more interesting than the straight walks along the ridges.

11H: White Sheet Hill across the valley to the Ox Drove

(8 miles: map 184):

After parking at White Sheet Quarry (934239), from east of White Sheet Hill on the Salisbury Way the head of the Ebble

Valley may be crossed by a footpath which leaves the Salisbury Way near a cross dyke at 948244 and runs down past Woodlands and a little east of Berwick St John. From the valley road east of this village (at 953223) the footpath already mentioned as the way followed by Monmouth after his defeat at Sedgemoor is followed up the east flank of Winkelbury to join the Ox Drove at 954207. After walking for a little over a mile west along the Ox Drove to Monk's Down the return is by the footpath north from 936207 through Berwick St John and north past Woodlands to White Sheet Hill.

11I: Bower Chalke from Cow Down Hill (4 miles: map 184):

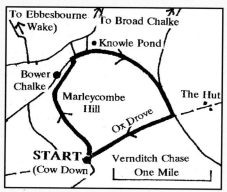

A fine walk over John Aubrey's countryside around Broad Chalke may be taken by parking on Cow Down Hill (023216) on the Ox Drove and walking north over Marleycombe Hill with its extensive earthworks and field systems and down the very steep descent into Bower Chalke. Here follow the footpath that runs north-east parallel to the village street and past Knowle Pond (025236) at Mead End which Aubrey considered to provide 'the best trouts in England' and is now appropriately a trout farm. From Knowle Pond swing south-east and follow the edge of the steep coombe west of Knowle Hill to the Ox Drove a little west of The Hut. The Ox Drove is then followed for a mile south-west back to Cow Down Hill.

11J: Broad Chalke to the Ox Drove (4.5 miles: map 184):

The Ox Drove may be reached from the Ebble Valley by parking beside the church at Broad Chalke and walking south-east up the gentle incline which passes round the head of a beautiful coombe on its way to the farm on Knighton Hill. The way then passes Knighton Earthworks (058238) – the Saxon *Wudu burh* – and continues south to the Ox Drove. After following the Ox Drove for half a mile south-westwards the return to Broad Chalke is north along the delightful Church Bottom or through

Middleton Down Nature Reserve which lies a little west of Church Bottom.

11K. Fovant Quarry to Broad Chalke (6 miles: map 184):
Aubrey's countryside may also be reached from the Salisbury Way by parking near Fovant Quarry south of Fovant (at 005274), walking east up the hollow-way to the Salisbury Way, crossing the way and continuing down the footpath which runs south-east over Knapp Down to Broad Chalke. The return route from Broad Chalke is north to the Salisbury Way on Compton Down and west past Chiselbury Camp.

11L. Bishopstone to the Ox Drove (5 miles: map 184):
Croucheston Drove, which leaves the Ox Drove at 067232, and Faulston Drove (from 081234) provide alternative descents northwards from the Ox Drove to Bishopstone in the Ebble Valley. A circular walk may be achieved by parking in Bishopstone and walking east through Faulston and up Faulston Drove to the Ox Drove which is then followed west to 067232. An alternative is to follow the Roman road south-west across the downs. From 067232 Croucheston Drove is followed north to Croucheston and Bishopstone.

11M. Bishopstone to the Salisbury Way (5 miles : map 184) :
The Salisbury Way may be reached from Bishopstone north up Bishopstone Drove (through 073272). The Salisbury Way is then followed for half a mile westwards, and from 063288 the path over Netton Down is followed south back to Bishopstone.

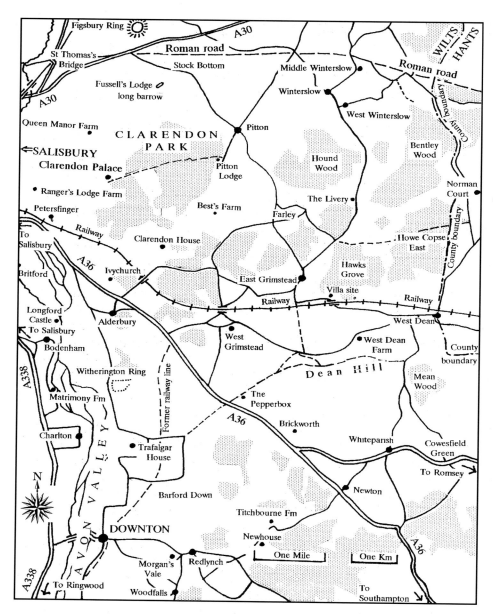

South-East Wiltshire

12 South-East Wiltshire

The Clarendon countryside east of and including the Salisbury Avon Valley

(map Landranger 184)

The area of Wiltshire described in this chapter – the extreme south-east of the county – lies east of the Salisbury Avon, which is sometimes known as the Hampshire Avon from the fact that after flowing south from Salisbury it crosses Hampshire to reach the sea near Christchurch. The northern boundary of the area is assumed to be the Roman road which runs east from Old Sarum to Winchester. Its southern and eastern limits are the county boundary with Hampshire.

The south-east of Wiltshire offers a varied terrain ranging from the lush river valley of the Salisbury Avon, to the wide open downlands north of Dean Hill which are interspersed with the extensive woodlands of Clarendon, Hound Wood, and Bentley Wood. South of Dean Hill more variety is provided by the area of broken woodland surviving from the Royal Forest of Clarendon which was effectively the extreme north-east part of the New Forest extending across south-east Wiltshire.

North of Dean Hill the geology of the arable lands consists of tertiary clays and sands overlying the chalk. At Dean Hill the chalk abruptly breaks through these deposits, but south of the hill the sands and clays reappear on a gentler incline to the south. Here a distinct change takes place in the appearance of the countryside. The woods become principally oak with hazel undergrowth, and these gradually give way to a New Forest type of vegetation at the northern extremity of the Hampshire Basin. Around Alderbury the Bagshot sandpits are associated with Scots pines which typify the New Forest vegetation.

Apart from its varied topography, this district offers a great number of historical associations. Its prehistory is rather lacking when compared to the dramatic archaeology of the great open downlands of Wiltshire, although several Roman villas have been found here, and its northern boundary has already been defined as the Roman road from Old Sarum (the Roman

Sorbiodunum) to Winchester (*Venta Belgarum*). This road is the continuation of the 'Lead Road' running from the Charterhouse lead mines in the Mendips to the south coast through Great Ridge Wood and Grovely Wood which was described in Chapter 9.

In early medieval times south-east Wiltshire became of great importance when England was often governed from the royal palace at Clarendon. The area was then extensively used for the deer-hunting that provided recreation for the early medieval kings and their courtiers. There are Civil War associations, and Charles II crossed south-east Wiltshire in his flight after being defeated at Worcester. Later there were projects for river navigation up the Avon, and for a canal to Salisbury from the south coast.

The Valley of the Salisbury Avon

Henry VIII's antiquary John Leland recorded that Salisbury was 'the pan or receyver of most part of the water of Wileshire'. At or near Salisbury five Wiltshire rivers – the Ebble, Nadder, Wylye, Avon and the Bourne – combine to run south across Hampshire and enter the sea near Christchurch. For some miles after leaving Salisbury the River Avon runs in numerous channels, and over this stretch walking beside the river is hazardous as the walker is liable to be cut off by these channels.

Britford

The first village in the Avon Valley south-east of Salisbury is Britford ('the ford of the Britons'), an ancient place with a church of Saxon foundation. Thin tiles, which may be Roman, are incorporated in an arch on the interior of the south side of the church. This district was of importance in Anglo-Saxon times when it was held by the king, Edward the Confessor. The *Anglo-Saxon Chronicle* recorded that in 1065 the Earl Tostig, the brother of the future King Harold, was at Britford with King Edward. Britford, which offers striking views of Salisbury cathedral,

Britford Church.

138

formerly had a flourishing sheep fair.

A monument in Britford church is dubiously claimed to be that of Henry Stafford, 2nd Duke of Buckingham (1455-1483) who was executed at Salisbury. Buckingham was the Chamberlain and Constable of England under the usurper Richard III. He was probably provoked into raising the south of England in rebellion against Richard in October 1483 out of fear at the insecure king's unscrupulous methods, and the dangers to which his own royal blood might expose him. Having fled north when deserted by his supporters, Buckingham was captured by the Sheriff of Shropshire who delivered him to Richard III at Salisbury where he was beheaded in Blue Boar Row on 2 November 1483, aged 28.

Longford Castle

Longford is an estate rather than a village, Longford Castle being situated in a 250-acre park beside the Avon a mile and a half south of Britford. The name Longford indicates that the river was forded at this point. Thomas Gorges (1536-1610) purchased the Longford estate in 1574 and in 1580 married the Swedish-born widow of the Marquis of Northampton. This lady induced her husband to build Longford Castle, it is said out of envy of nearby Wilton House which was being developed on the site of the former abbey by the Herberts following the Dissolution of the Monasteries. Longford remained obscure, although it provided the model for the 'Castle of Amphialeus' of Sir Philip Sidney's *Arcadia* (1580).

Longford Castle, which bears the date of its completion in 1591, was built to a triangular plan with a triangular hall at its core and circular towers at every apex, on a site associated with the old Norman hunting family of Waleran. The towers give the house some resemblence to a medieval castle and during the Civil War Longford for a short while functioned as a castle, being garrisoned by Royalist cavalry in 1644. In 1645 it was besieged and surrendered to Cromwell, but was for some reason spared from the destruction which was the usual penalty for such resistance.

The present owners of Longford are the Earls of Radnor, a title borne by the Robartes family from 1657 to 1757 and subsequently by the Pleydell-Bouveries. They bought Longford in 1717 and William Bouverie, a prosperous Huguenot, was created the first Baron Longford (1747) and Earl of Radnor (1765). His son Jacob assumed the name of Pleydell-Bouverie. Helen, Countess of Radnor founded and conducted a small orchestra for which Sir Hubert Parry (1848-1918), who had married into the Pembrokes of Wilton, in 1894 wrote his Lady Radnor Suite.

Longford Castle is in private grounds and is not accessible to walkers, although it is overlooked from The Pepperbox at the west end of Dean Hill. A footpath from Britford to Alderbury crosses the Avon a little north of Longford Castle near Bullock's Hole Farm.

Alderbury

The village of Alderbury stands on the hill at the east flank of the Avon Valley, opposite Longford Castle with distant views of Salisbury Cathedral spire. Alderbury House was built with masonry salvaged from the campanile of Salisbury Cathedral after its demolition by Wyatt in the late-18th century. A little north of Alderbury lay the Norman Priory of Ivychurch, described later under Clarendon Palace, which it served.

Alderbury is associated with Charles Dickens who described his Blue Dragon inn in *Martin Chuzzlewit* as situated 'in a little Wiltshire village within an easy journey of the fair old town of Salisbury'. It is generally accepted that the 'Blue Dragon' was based on the Green Dragon at Alderbury where Dickens stayed while collecting material for his book. The local writer Ralph Whitlock could recall talking to an elderly lady who had ferried Dickens across the Avon.

At Bodenham, immediately south of Longford Castle, the Avon is joined by the River Ebble. Here a minor road runs beside a particularly beautiful stretch of the river, past a farm with the intriguing name of Matrimony Farm.

Trafalgar House

The hamlet of Charlton provides fine views across the valley of the Avon and into the New Forest. Opposite Charlton, above the east bank of the river, stands Trafalgar House, a Georgian red-brick mansion, designed in 1733 by Roger Morris for the banker Sir Peter Vanderput. It was formerly known as Standlynch, but acquired its present name from the fact that after Lord Nelson's death at the Battle of Trafalgar in 1805 a grateful nation presented

it to his elder brother, the Rev. William Nelson, when he was created Earl Nelson of Trafalgar. Nelson would no doubt have preferred the estate

Alderbury fountain, built using columns from Ivychurch Priory. Green Dragon Inn right.

to be bestowed upon Lady Hamilton. The Trafalgar estate was sold by the 5th Earl Nelson in the 1940s and in 1995 Trafalgar House – by then in desperate need of repair – was bought by Mr Michael Wade who hopes to turn it into a centre for emerging young musicians.

An amusing story is told about the reaction of the gardener at Alderbury when bones were found buried near Trafalgar House. He suggested that the find was hardly surprising as he had once been told that a great battle had been fought at Trafalgar!

River Avon at Bodenham.

Downton

The last village on the Salisbury Avon before it enters Hampshire at Charford is Downton, a large village extending west to east across the several streams of the Avon but situated principally on the east bank.

The Romans built a villa at Downton (at 181210) on a spur projecting south-west on a terrace on the east side of the Avon. Excavation in 1953-7 established that it was of the linear corridor type with a range of seven rooms lying east of the corridor and a bath house at its southern end. All the rooms except the bath house had tesselated floors and the room at the centre of the range had a decorative mosaic floor.

From the third quarter of the 7th century AD the manor of Downton belonged to the Bishops of Winchester. Henry de Blois – Bishop of Winchester and a grandson of William I – built a castle here (at 181213) which was plundered in 1147. At the east end of Downton in the garden of a private house is The Moot, a Saxon earthwork that was a place of assembly.

Downton used to have a market and two fairs for livestock, one in April and one in October. The markets and the October fair, which was principally for sheep and New Forest ponies, are no longer held, but the April fair is still held and is known as Downton Cuckoo Fair because it generally coincides with the arrival of the cuckoo. Local people used to claim that on April 12th they opened the Forest gate at Downton to allow the cuckoo through!

The Saxon Conquest

In the early 6th century, at the time when the former Romano-Britain was being taken over by Saxon invaders, an army of Saxons led by Cerdic and Cynric expanded northwards, having landed at *Cerdics-ora* on the south coast in 495. In their gradual advance up the Avon Valley they in 519 reached *Cerdicesford* – now Charford on the Wiltshire-Hampshire border – and there they fought a decisive battle with the Britons. The *Anglo-Saxon Chronicle* recorded:

> 519. In this year Cerdic and Cynric obtained the kingdom of the West Saxons, and in the same year they fought against the Britons at a place now called *Cerdicesford*. And from that day on the princes of the West Saxons have reigned.

The victors then established the kingdom of Wessex (West Saxons) with its capital at Wilton. Its people became known as the *Wilsaetas*, a name which means the dwellers on the Wylye.

The Salisbury Avon Navigation

In the days when roads were dreadful and waterways were an important means of carrying goods, the poet John Taylor in 1623 suggested that the Salisbury Avon should be made navigable from Christchurch, on the south coast, to Salisbury. For many years nothing was done, but in 1664 the River Navigation Act was passed by Parliament allowing the improvement of the Avon from Christchurch to Salisbury and the Wylye from Salisbury to Wilton to make them more navigable. Another period of inactivity followed, until in 1675 the Mayor and Corporation of Salisbury decided to start work on the project. A printed paper dated 1675 concluded that 'the City [Salisbury] which depends now for its subsistence upon an Inn-land Trade, and the Western Road, will acquire the reputation of a Port; and in the Catalogue of the Cities of this Kingdom, be rank'd with Bristoll'. Work began in September 1675, and continued until 1677 when money ran out and the project was abandoned.

In 1685 this project, that might have made Salisbury an inland port, was revived. Surviving documents suggest that by 1688 the Avon was navigable by means of 'severall Locks, Turnepikes Cutts and other works, raysed, built made and done in or neare the said river and a New Haven' (presumably at Christchurch). Work continued in a merely desultory way, but the Avon seems never to have been made fully navigable, and the project was finally abandoned in about 1730. Few signs of the works survive except for a lock at Britford (159278).

The Salisbury Canal

About a hundred years later a proposal was advertised in the *Salisbury Journal* (21 August 1770) for a Southampton to Salisbury canal to cross this area. The proposed route was from Salisbury along the Dean Valley, joining the Andover Canal at Kimbridge mill. It was also proposed that the canal be extended up the Wylye Valley to Warminster. This scheme was destined to enjoy even less success than the earlier Salisbury Avon Navigation. Construction began in 1795 but never reached Salisbury. A combination of flooding, poor workmanship, lack of money, and the outbreak of war – in 1775 with the American colonists and in 1778 with France and Spain –

West Dean village.

prevented progress beyond Alderbury, and the Andover Canal scheme failed in 1772 to achieve approval by Parliament. Some traffic betwen West Grimstead and Dunbridge on the River Test took place until 1808 when traffic finally ceased. By 1834 landowners were filling in the canal excavation to regain their property, and local people were raiding the works for building materials. Traces of this canal may still be seen at West Dean where the canal entered Wiltshire from Hampshire. Here the canal wharf stands in front of the Red Lion public house and gives the village something of the character of an inland port. The only original bridge over the canal survives as a three-arched bridge (225272) a short distance south of East Grimstead church, and the main survival is the deep cutting for the canal at Alderbury (193268) which was excavated in two sections but never connected by its proposed tunnel.

Prehistoric Antiquities

As a consequence of the forested character of much of the landscape, Prehistoric remains in this extreme south-east corner of Wiltshire are less profuse than in the open downlands. The Neolithic Fussell's Lodge long barrow (192324) stands a little south of the Roman road at Stock Bottom, and a number of Bronze Age round barrows are scattered in the woodlands, with a particular group near Hamptworth Lodge (231193).

The Iron Age fortresses of Figsbury Ring and Clearbury Ring lie slightly outside the area defined for this chapter, respectively to its north and west. Witherington Ring (185252), south of Alderbury and the only Iron Age enclosure within the area, has been neglected by virtually all commentators on the archaeology of Wessex.

The surviving Roman antiquities – the Old Sarum to Winchester road and several Roman villas – will be mentioned later.

Clarendon Palace

The principal historic feature of this district is found among the woods east of Salisbury. This is the now deserted remains of the great Palace of Clarendon, one of the most significant and yet unregarded medieval archaeological sites of Wiltshire, or indeed of England. It is situated on the edge of the Royal Forest of Clarendon, on a north-facing hill with noble views two miles east of Salisbury, which did not exist when the palace was founded.

Exploratory shafts sunk through the ruins of the palace have revealed an earlier building of Saxon or Norman date, although the earliest medieval building on the site is believed to have been a hunting lodge in Clarendon Forest of uncertain date. A palace may have been developed on this wooded site, remote from water, to replace Wilton Palace which was pillaged and destroyed by Sweyn in the 9th century. By the Conqueror's time Clarendon had become a place of importance and before he went to Scotland in 1072 William I summoned his troops to gather here.

A later event of great importance in the history of England occurred here twenty years after the Norman Conquest in 1086. As a consequence of having suffered two rebellions by his Norman subjects the king – when at Old Sarum presumably for the hunting at Clarendon – summoned all the landowners of England to a 'Grand Gemote'. At this time the countries of Europe all consisted of loose associations of many practically independent states. Here, in August 1086, King William required all the landowners to swear an oath of fealty to him 'against all other men' rather than to their overlords. By this means William effectively united England under its monarch, although he himself died in Normandy the following month (September 1086).

The palace at Clarendon gradually became a very important place. For its time it was unusual in being practically unfortified, the garrison at the Norman castle of Old Sarum being within easy call only three miles to the north-west. There was a precinct wall and a ditch enclosing 75 acres of which some signs remain. After the murder in 1312 of his favourite, Piers Gaveston, Edward II is known to have distracted himself with the manual labour of digging, and is said to have literally helped to dig the ditch around Clarendon.

The Norman and Angevin kings were itinerant, moving from palace to palace, taking their government with them whilst enjoying the pleasures of the chase. From the time (1087-1100) of William Rufus the successive monarchs were frequently at Clarendon for the hunting. Parliament would sometimes assemble here, and affairs of state would be carried on during the royal visits. By about 1130 Clarendon was a regular royal habitation, and records of a visit by Henry II and his queen in 1170 survive. Henry II and Henry III – who was born at Winchester – both upgraded Clarendon and maintained the great cellar known as 'La Roche' which Henry II had started. Clarendon Palace became the second palace to Westminster in the kingdom, and the principal palace to have hunting readily available from it.

A great deer park, the largest in Wiltshire, was developed around the palace, and Clarendon became a favourite resort of the Plantagenet kings at the time that New Sarum was developing to its west and replacing Old Sarum. The Court would remain at Clarendon often for a month, sometimes longer. Then Clarendon would be left for long spells, before being again put into repair for another visit by the Court. Like most medieval palaces, Clarendon was not planned. It just grew as needs changed and additional apartments

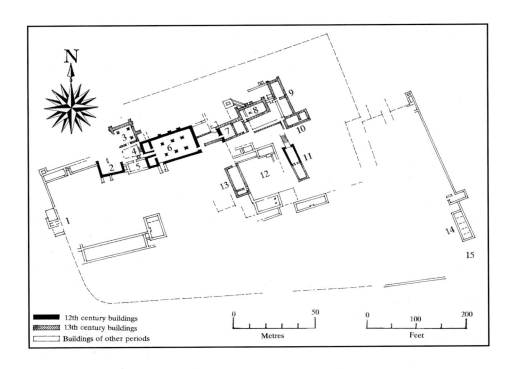

0   50

Metres

0   100   200

Feet

Above: Reconstructed Plan of Clarendon Palace
Key: 1 Great West Gate (to Salisbury); 2 West (Household) Kitchen; 3 North (King's) Kitchen; 4 Cloister; 5 Salsary (Larder); 6 Great Hall; 7 King's Chambers; 8 Antioch Chamber; 9 Queen's Chambers; 10 Chapel; 11 Great Wine Cellar ('La Roche'); 12 Courtyard Garden; 13 Chamber of Alexander (?); 14 Barn; 15 Site of East Gateway (to Winchester).

Left: Clarendon Palace, remains of the east end of the Great Hall, known as the 'Protestant Fragment'.

were casually added as the necessity arose for them.

In 1164 a council was held at Clarendon at which the sixteen-point Constitutions of Clarendon were evolved to re-affirm the power of the king over the Church and limit the excessive power of the clergy. This led to the break between Henry II and his 'troublesome priest' Thomas à Becket, his Archbishop of Canterbury, a dispute that culminated in the latter's martyrdom at Canterbury in 1170. Salisbury's first charter was granted by Henry III when he was at Clarendon in 1227, and here, after the Black Prince won his great victory at the Battle of Poitiers (1356) during the prolongued French wars, four kings – Edward III of England, his prisoner John of France, Henry of Navarre, and David of Scotland – took part in a royal hunt whilst lodged at Clarendon. Sir Roger of Clarendon, the illegitimate son of the Black Prince who was killed in 1402 by order of Henry IV who feared his claim to the throne as Richard II's half brother, was born here. Tilting tournaments were frequently held at Clarendon up to the time that Henry VIII neglected this palace in favour of his newer and more accessible palaces at Hampton Court, Nonesuch, Sheen, and Greenwich.

The palace covered about 18 acres, and was probably principally single-storeyed, although a comparison between the number of rooms comprising the royal apartments described in documents with the ground plan of this suite as reconstructed by excavation suggests that this part of the palace at least was two-storeyed. Henry III loved fine art and employed the foremost masters and craftsmen at Clarendon. During his time there was a Great Hall, king's and queen's apartments, several chapels, kitchens, offices and more. The Great Hall measured only 83 feet by 51 feet (25.3m by 15.5m) with two four-bay arcades, and was second only to Westminster Hall in splendour. Built in 1358-9 in Chilmark stone, it was columned and aisled, with three doors leading to buttery, pantry, and kitchen corridor. It was entered by a south porch built in 1244. During the reign of Henry VI a separate block of kitchens was added. The buildings were principally of flint with, from the evidence that survives, few stone dressings. Brick was also used, in thin tile-like form resembling Roman brick, often used in herring-bone pattern. This represents one of the earliest medieval uses of brick in England since Roman times and raises the question: could there have been a Roman building on the site which was quarried to supply these bricks? The site abounded in medieval glazed encaustic tiles. Some of these tiles were imported from France (Henry III had married Eleanor of Provence) but many were fired in a 13th century kiln on the palace site. Many of the decorative floor tiles found at Clarendon bear representations of stylised animals and birds, some have mounted knights. Others have patterns, and a few the fleur-de-lys of France. These tiles have now all been removed to museums for it was their theft by souvenir hunters that has led the owner to make the site of Clarendon Palace private land.

The circular tiled pavement in the king's chapel incorporated an inscription which proudly declared in Latin that it was the pavement of Henry, King of England. The palace must have resembled a village, with many detached buildings clustered around the great banqueting hall like cottages around a church.

The Norman kings maintained palaces at both Winchester and Westminster and used Winchester, situated merely eighteen miles east of Clarendon, as their capital. This undoubtedly contributed to the popularity of Clarendon, but under Henry III's son Edward III, who reigned 1272-1307, London superseded Winchester as the capital and the fortunes of Clarendon declined with those of Winchester. During the Wars of the Roses the palace at Clarendon fell into disuse and disrepair. Henry V so far as is known seldom visited Clarendon, and neither Henry VII nor Henry VIII considered it worth repairing, although during the reign of Henry VII a Clerk of Works was still employed here. The last king to reside at Clarendon was probably Henry VI who in 1453 was overtaken by one of his fits of insanity there, and was unable to dine in the Great Hall with the rest of the Court. The last building work at Clarendon appears to have been a special suite built to accommodate this king and his attendants.

When, in 1574, Queen Elizabeth visited Clarendon with a hunting party while visiting the Earl of Pembroke at Wilton, the buildings were so decayed that temporary arbours had to be erected to accommodate the royal party for lunch.

The decline continued. Woods grew up through the ruins which were quarried for building materials, and the site was almost forgotten for centuries although William Stukeley sketched what survived in 1723 and recorded that 'Part of the building is still left, tho they have been pulling it down many years. 'Tis chiefly of flint and was a large place upon the side of a hill, but no way fortifyd'. The Andrews and Dury map of Wiltshire (1773) marked Clarendon as 'Ruins of King John's House' and also showed Queen's Lodge' – now Queen's Manor Farm – one mile north of the palace site. The decline of Clarendon was shared by the decline of its associated castle at Old Sarum.

Also associated with Clarendon Palace was a large royal deer park – the largest in Wiltshire – which provided meat, skins, and hunting for the Court when it was at Clarendon, and later after the palace had been abandoned. As early as 1223 Clarendon Park was surrounded by a timber park-pale and in 1650, long after the palace was abandoned, 4293 acres were enclosed. A plan showing the bounds of the park in 1650 is reproduced in Volume 4 (page 455) of the *Victoria County History of Wiltshire*. Charles I mortgaged the park in 1637 and after the Restoration in 1665 Clarendon Park finally went out of Crown ownership when Charles II granted it to George Monk, Earl of Albemarle, who had brought about his Restoration.

Between 1933 and 1939 the site of Clarendon Palace was excavated by Dr Tancred Borenius, the Finnish art historian who resided in London. The excavation extended over an area of 750 feet by 300 feet (229m by 91m) and confirmed the former existence of a palace which resembled a small town. The excavation generated much interest and the visitors' book reveals a broad spectrum of visitors including an impecunious German student called Nikolaus Pevsner (later the author of 'The Buildings of England' series) who is said to have borrowed his fare back to London. The work was interrupted by the war, and the death of Dr Borenius in 1948 put a final end to the work. His excavations were filled, and the site again reverted to nature, although more excavations were undertaken in the 1960s and substantial foundations are still visible and the form of the palace may still be seen on the ground.

Until recently the remains of the palace were covered with woods, but when I last visited the site in October 1997 many of the trees and much of their undergrowth had been cleared away. Apart from a crag of ivy-capped flint walling about nine metres high – formerly the north-east corner of the Great Hall – little remains other than foundation walls. This surviving section of walling became known to the excavators in the 1930s as the 'Protestant Fragment' from the fact that when its owner, Sir Frederick Bathurst, in 1844 consolidated it he placed on the wall a carved stone inscription suggesting that the Constitutions of Clarendon of 1164 represented one of the earliest manifestations of Protestantism in England. The Great Hall and its internal columns are well-defined on the ground, and the steps leading down into the great royal wine cellar known as 'Le Roche' are still visible. The flint walls of the corridor from the kitchens into the west end of the Great Hall also survive to a height of about four feet (1.2m). The bank and ditch marking the line of the former precinct wall may still be seen.

Because of its extreme sensitivity visitors to the site are deterred by many 'Keep Out' signs, but a well-trodden footpath – part of The Clarendon Way – runs south-west to north-east across Clarendon Park and passes close to the palace ruins. Applications for permission to enter the site should be addressed to the Clarendon Estate Office at Salisbury.

Clarendon Palace is one of the most evocative places to be found in Wiltshire, an example of a great royal palace now ruined and reclaimed by nature. In 1801 John Britton wrote of Clarendon: 'The habitation of kings is levelled with the dust ; and all the proud revelry of a Court has now given way to the hooting of the owl and the croaking of the raven. Nothing remains of its former magnificence but ruined walls and heaps of rubbish', and in the Wiltshire volume of 'The Buildings of England' Sir Nikolaus Pevsner pleaded for Clarendon: 'One crag of walling stands up. All the rest is back to its sleeping beauty. Surely, out of respect for English history if for no other reason, these remains ought to be as clearly visible as those of Old Sarum'.

Ivychurch Priory

The spiritual needs of the Court when at Clarendon were provided for by the Augustinian Priory of Ivychurch situated a mile and a half south of Clarendon and no longer linked to it by public footpath. Ivychurch Priory – the Ivied Priory, built in the 12th century in the time of King Stephen – was the Monastery of Hederose in an Assize Roll of 1224 (*Hedera* is the Latin name for ivy). Its establishment was a prior and thirteen canons, of whom all but one called James de Groundewell died in the Black Death of 1348-9. He then opportunistically applied for the post of prior and obtained it, but himself died within the year!

The martyr Thomas à Beckett lodged at Ivychurch at the time when the Constitions of Clarendon were being formulated and used to walk from here to Clarendon Palace. After Ivychurch had declined to secular use it was leased to Henry, Earl of Pembroke. The Pembrokes made a dwelling house out of the priory and Aubrey tells us that 'Mary, Countess of Pembroke, much delighted in this place' [Ivychurch], and that her brother Sir Philip Sidney 'spent much, if not most, of his time at Wilton and at Ivychurch near Salisbury, which did then belong to his family', but at the beginning of the 19th century it was bought by the Earl of Radnor. For a time it functioned as a school but

in 1888 the priory was finally demolished and very little of the ancient building remains.

From a little road which loops east of the road through Alderbury the ruins of the Priory of

Remains of Ivychurch Priory. Norman columns, arches and fragments built into farmhouse.

Ivychurch are accessible by a lane which diverges from a farm drive. One scallop-headed Norman column and the springing of the arches of an arcade survive *in situ* together with a later pointed doorway and an ancient looking wall. Some other fragments are built into an adjoining farmhouse. The village drinking fountain at Alderbury, built by Lord Radnor in 1897, utilised four pairs of Norman capitals from Ivychurch.

Pitton and Farley

Immediately east of Clarendon Park lie the villages of Pitton and Farley. Pitton was the birthplace and for most of his life the home of the farmer, writer and broadcaster Ralph Whitlock (1914-1995), an authority on this part of Wiltshire. He is perhaps best remembered for his BBC Children's Hour radio programmes 'Cowleaze Farm' which ran from 1945-1962.

Ralph Whitlock, who came from a family of Wiltshire shepherds and farmers, was a man of small stature and great charm. He started writing during the Depression when, as a schoolboy, he discovered that the local papers paid a halfpenny a line for copy. It is said that he sometimes tripled his income from writing by taking carbon copies and sending the same copy to three newspapers! He became a prolific writer, generally on country matters, and also farming editor to *The Field*. Ralph Whitlock regularly provided articles to the *Guardian Weekly*, from which selections were collected for his *Letters from an English Village* (1988) and *Letters from the English Countryside* (1992). His ardent Methodism took him to Africa, India and the Caribbean as a consultant to the Methodist Missionary Society. He was also a founder and trustee of the Bentley Wood Trust which cares for Bentley Wood, situated on the county boundary east of Pitton and Farley. Ralph Whitlock was buried at Pitton church after a service at Pitton Methodist chapel.

The neighbouring village to Pitton is Farley, a tiny village with a most imposing grouping of church and almshouses. Its name derives from *fearn-leah*, meaning 'bracken clearing'. The church and almshouses owe their existence to the generosity of Sir Stephen Fox who came from a long-established local family and himself recorded that he was born 'in a cottage at Ffareley in Wiltshire'.

Sir Stephen Fox

By the early 1650s Mr Stephen Fox (1627-1716) was sufficiently in favour with Charles II to share his exile. After the Restoration he continued in high favour and was knighted in 1665 and made Paymaster General to the Forces. In this capacity he projected Chelsea Hospital for old soldiers, and in 1680 he was one of the Lord Commisioners of the Treasury. In his diary for 6 September 1680 John Evelyn wrote of Sir Stephen :

> This gentleman came first a poor boy from the choir of Salisbury... his Majesty being in exile, and Mr Fox waiting, both the King and Lords about him frequently employed him about their affairs, and trusted him both with receiving and paying the little money they had.

Evelyn then describes how Sir Stephen returned to England at the Restoration and revealed such dexterity in handling money that he obtained preferment and was 'believed to be worth at least £200,000, honestly got and unenvied'. Sir Stephen continued his career in politics and became paymaster to William III. In 1670 he began to buy up estates in the Farley area and in 1678 purchased the lease of the Manor of Pitton and Farley from the cathedral authorities. From his fortune he funded the almshouses opposite the church, founded in 1682 for three old men and three old women. A few years later he built Farley church to replace the original rustic church of flint and thatch that had been built in 1190 about 300 yards west of the present church in Chapel Close. No signs of the old church survive.

The almshouses are designed in a homely vernacular style appropriate

to their function, but Farley church is built in a rather ponderous Baroque classical style which is in marked contrast to the elegant soaring Gothic of Salisbury cathedral; and yet this church at Farley has a certain distinction, apart from its curiosity value as a classical church. It is clear from the Wren Society papers that Alexander Fort (died 1706) – the Master Joiner at the Office of Works – was responsible for the design of the Farley almshouses, and it seems likely that he also provided the design for Farley church, although the church probably owes its classical style to Sir Stephen's friendship with another

Classical church at Farley.

Wiltshireman, Sir Christopher Wren, who had designed Chelsea Hospital and at the time that the church at Farley was built was busy supervising the building of St Paul's Cathedral in London.

Sir Stephen's eldest son was in 1756 created Earl of Ilchester. The family maintained their connection with this district and both the Earl and his wife, who were the parents of the politician Charles James Fox, were buried at Farley in 1774. Farley church contains an imposing monument to Sir Stephen Fox, and a tablet commemorating his grandson Charles James Fox.

Winterslow and William Hazlitt

The Pheasant Inn, situated on the A30 some distance north of the Winterslow villages, was formerly a coaching inn known as Winterslow Hut. This establishment provides an example of an inn developing from one of the humble 'Huts' of south Wiltshire (mentioned in Chapter 11). These 'Huts' had originally provided simple fare for ordinary travellers. An incident occurred at Winterslow Hut in October 1816 when a lioness escaped from a travelling menagerie and attacked the coach horses of the Exeter mail. The incident was illustrated in a well-known contemporary print.

Winterslow Hut was associated with the critic and essayist William Hazlitt (1778-1830) who in 1808 married a Miss Stoddart from Winterslow. They settled in a cottage in this village, but the marriage did not long survive. Hazlitt had however grown fond of the district and continued to work at the Winterslow Hut where he wrote his *Winterslow Essays*. Despite their title these essays have little to say about Winterslow, being an arbitrary posthumous collection made in 1839 by Hazlitt's son. *The Life of Napoleon* (1828-30), Hazlitt's last major work, was also written at Winterslow.

Hazlitt left us one of the best essays on the joys of walking in the essay 'On Going a Journey':

> I go out of town in order to forget the town and all that is in it   Give me the clear blue sky over my head, and the green turf beneath my feet, a winding road before me, and three hour's march to dinner – and then to thinking! Then long-forgotten things burst upon my eager sight, and I begin to feel, think, and be myself again

A glimpse into the life of Hazlitt at Winterslow is provided by this quotation from his works :

> I used to walk out with Mr and Mrs Lamb of an evening, to look at the Claude Lorraine skies over our heads melting from azure into purple

and gold, and to gather mushrooms, that sprang up at our feet, to throw into our hashed mutton at supper,

and in the preface to the *Winterslow Essays* Hazlitt's son recorded of his father that: 'One of his chief attractions hither were the noble woods of Tytherleigh or Tudorleigh, round Norman Court' – presumably Bentley Wood which lies immediately west of West Tytherley as no Tytherley Woods appear on the modern map.

Truffle-hunting at Winterslow

Winterslow was one of the last strongholds of the now recently revived practice of truffle-hunting in England. Truffles were an expensive delicacy and a long established and lively trade existed in this commodity – a fungus found near the surface, particularly in beech and oak woods. They were found by using trained dogs known as truffle hounds.

The last truffle hunters in England lived at Jubilee Cottage at Winterslow. Eli Collins, who continued to search for truffles until he was 83, was succeeded by his son Alfred who practised truffling until the 1930s and died as recently as 1953. His father was so famous that it is said that letters adressed 'Eli Collins, Truffle Hunter, Salisbury Plain' were safely delivered. Truffle-hunting was a winter activity carried on from November to mid March, so that during the rest of the year both father and son had summer employment as woodmen in the woods around Winterslow.

Many truffles were found on the Longford Estate, and the Earl of Radnor provided the following testimonial for Eli Collins, who often worked far afield in Southern England:

> Eli Collins had been allowed to hunt for truffles on my Estate for nearly 45 years, commencing to do so with his father – he has never during that time encroached in any way; and has always conducted himself respectably. Aug 22 1898.

The truffle spikes with which the Collins family dug up their truffles are now in Salisbury Museum.

Norman Court and Celia Fiennes

Norman Court provides another literary asociation with this area. The house, which actually stands just over the Wiltshire boundary in Hampshire, three miles south-east of Winterslow and adjoining Bentley Wood, is associated with Celia Fiennes (1662-1741), that bold lady traveller who rode side-saddle over the appalling roads of 17th century England from Land's End to the Scottish border. Her impressions of the country were first published in 1888 as *Through England on a Side Saddle in the Time of William and Mary*. Later editions appeared after 1947 under the title *The Journeys of Celia Fiennes*. Between 1685 and 1703 Celia Fiennes travelled in every county in England. She was the grand-daughter of the First Viscount Saye and Sele and the daughter of Colonel Nathaniel Fiennes (1608-1669).

Civil War and Commonwealth

No major Civil War action took part in this area, although towards the end of 1644 it was briefly a centre of operations. In October of that year Charles I marched east out of Devonshire, intending to destroy Parliament's forces in the south of England. On 15 October he entered Salisbury and Sir William Waller marched west against him, but was unsupported by the other Parliamentary commanders. On 25 October the indecisive Second Battle of Newbury was fought. There was then much activity in Hampshire which spilled over into the adjoining area of south-east Wiltshire. In December 1644 two troops of Parliamentary cavalry under Major Dowett and Major Wansey were billeted with eighty prisoners at West Dean House and the following month (January 1645) Lord Goring was at Whiteparish with 3000 Royalist horse, 1500 infantry and an artillery train. The dashing and unprincipled Goring succeeded in driving Waller out of Andover and by 9 January 1645 had advanced as far east as Farnham but, realising that he had ventured too far and become detached, fell back to Salisbury committing his normal 'horrid outrages' including his normal practice of extortion by holding local dignitaries to ransom.

Although the Church authorities remained staunchly Royalist many of the local landowners sided with Parliament, including Sir John Evelyn of West Dean, and Colonel Richard Whitehead (1594-1663) who owned the vast estates of of Norman Court and was the grandfather of Celia Fiennes. In her journals Celia Fiennes wrote of 'a good old Seate of Mr Whiteheads, my Grandfathers, Normans Court in West Tytherly', and also proudly noted that her three Whitehead uncles and her five Fienne uncles all fought against the king in the Civil War. Colonel Fiennes was never reconciled to Charles II and died in obscurity.

Flight of Charles II

During his flight after the Battle of Worcester – which took place on 3 September 1651 – Prince Charles, later Charles II – moved east on 13 October from Heale House in the valley of the Avon near Middle Woodford where he had been in hiding for several days. In fleeing east he hoped to embark from Sussex to France. At this time Charles was a young man of 20 and his disguise must have posed particular problems because, in an age when men were generally short, he was very tall. Parliament's 'wanted' notices described him as 'A tall, black man [he was of dark complexion], six feet two inches high'.

The precise route of Prince Charles's flight south-east is not known. According to one account the party fled 'past Old Sarum and Clarendon park corner, across the downland dome of eastern Wiltshire to Tytherley and the Test valley at Mottisfont'. A flight past Clarendon, which he knew well, seems inevitable, and local lore supports this route. According to one story Charles and his party were surprised by Parliamentary cavalry near Farley and hid in 'Dean Hedge' which still exists between Farley and The Livery (238297). He finally escaped to the Continent from Shoreham harbour on 15 October.

It is of interest to speculate whether Sir Stephen Fox gained favour with Charles II by assisting him in his flight across this hostile area. At the time Stephen Fox was aged 24 and had, during the campaign that led up to the Battle of Worcester, been responsible under Lord Percy for the supervision of Prince Charles's ordnance. *The Dictionary of National Biography* states positively that Stephen Fox 'took an active part in assisting the escape of Charles to Normandy'.

Four years later, during the 1655 Penruddocke rising against Parliament which took place in south Wiltshire, Sir John Wagstaff assembled sixty mounted troopers in Clarendon Park, led them to Salisbury, and joined Colonel Penruddocke in arresting the Sheriff and the judges on circuit in a failed attempt to restore the monarchy.

Dean Hill

At the very heart of the area described in this chapter is Dean Hill, the low long-ridged hill which runs at a height of about 500 feet (152m) west to east across this district. This impressive hill runs east from the A36 near West Grimstead into Hampshire. Dean Hill, with its patchwork of yew, whitebeam and beech, is a glorious sight in spring when the sombreness of the yew makes a striking contrast with the fresh translucent green of the emerging beech foliage and the paleness of the whitebeam. The yew, which is not generally common in the wild in Wiltshire, proliferates here on the Hampshire boundary. In Hampshire yew was so common that it was known as the 'Hampshire weed', just as the elm was known as the 'Wiltshire weed' prior to the devastations caused by the Dutch elm disease.

The now lost continuation of the Ox Drove ridgeway (described in Chapter 11) must have crossed this area and may have run on east over Wick Down and forded the Salisbury Avon at Downton, in which case it would have continued through Whiteparish. However, if it retained its character as a ridgeway following high ground, the Ox Drove may have veered north-east, crossed the Avon at Charlton, and run on into Hampshire along the ridge of Dean Hill. This seems to be a more probable route than a more southerly one through the woodlands on the edge of the New Forest.

The road under Dean Hill (left) looking west.

Beneath Dean Hill a delightful road runs west from West Dean on the Hampshire border and through West Grimstead. It passes through a copse of beeches (243265) which straddle the road west of West Dean, before reaching Dean Hill Farm – 'Deane Farm' on Andrews and Dury's 1773 map – a fine farm with a multitude of mossy-tiled roofs now augmented by metal-clad barns. The buildings of Dean Hill Farm are the only buildings on this road over its four mile stretch from West Dean to West Grimstead.

The writer Edward Thomas (1878-1917) was an admirer of Dean Hill which reminded him of the similar Shoulder of Mutton Hill near his home at Steep in Hampshire with which he identified so strongly. He made a point of coming along the Dean Valley in 1913 on the cycle ride from London to the Quantocks which he described in his travel book *In Pursuit of Spring* (1914), the book that finally transformed Thomas from prose writer to poet: 'Above all, I wanted to ride along under Dean Hill, the level-ridged chalk hill dotted with yew that is seen running parallel to the railway a quarter mile on your left as you near Salisbury from Eastleigh'.

Pepperbox Hill, at the west end of Dean Hill above the A36 Salisbury to Southampton road, obtains its name from Eyre's Folly, the octogonal brick building which was built in 1606 by one of the Eyre family as a gazebo from which the deer-hunting could be watched in the valley below. It appeared in the 1773 map by Andrews and Dury as 'Summer House', on the old one-inch Ordnance Survey as 'Eyre's Folly', and on the modern map as 'The Pepperbox'. The Eyre family owned Brickworth, and a member of this family, Giles Eyre who died in 1655 and is commemorated by a monument at the west end of Whiteparish church, was in 1640 imprisoned for resisting illegal forced loans levied by Charles I.

A particularly straight droveway runs south from East Grimstead across the valley of Dean Brook and approaches Dean Hill from the north. The fact that this droveway is not shown on the 1773 map suggests that it was made after that date. From it, a little south of East Grimstead church, the immense cutting made for the railway through the chalk may be viewed. At the foot of Dean Hill this drove, rather than taking the hill head-on, branches, a way slanting up the hill in each direction from the West Dean to West Grimstead road to join the ridgeway. The spaciousness of the arable land north of Dean Hill is emphasised by the description of the Hampshire-based archaeologist Heywood Sumner: 'a straight drove-way between old thorn hedges leads across open arable land, where a tractor plough can drive a mile-long furrow without turning, towards East Grimstead village – across the Southern Railway, and the derelict canal.' This plain north of Dean Hill was for long desecrated by overhead power lines and pylons but during the late 1990s these were removed, much enhancing the appearance of the hill with its hanging woods.

The Dean Valley Roman Villas and Heywood Sumner

Heywood Sumner (1853-1940) came to this district just before the Great War to excavate the Roman villa at East Grimstead, which had been discovered from crop marks in a very dry summer. He was pleased to avail himself of the opportunity to excavate here because, as he pointed out, no Roman villa had been found in the entire New Forest.

There is a tendency to regard Roman villas as luxurious houses of the very rich. Where villas occur in rural districts they were often essentially working agricultural establishments – the Latin word *villa* means farm – and most Romano-British villas were working economic units producing for home consumption for the occupants and the labour force and a surplus for trading. Their distribution normally coincides with rich lowland arable areas.

The East Grimstead villa was a far more elaborate example than the Downton villa described earlier for it had three detached bath houses, a fact which led Heywood Sumner to speculate about the extravagant provision of three bath houses in a villa of this modest size. He came to the conclusion that such luxury must be attributed to human nature as displayed by the child who, when asked if his helping of pudding was too much, replied 'I like too much'!

The flush of Roman villas in the Dean Valley north of Dean Hill prompted Heywood Sumner's remark: 'Evidently the Roman settlers regarded the Dean Brook valley as desirable for occupation'. The Romans extensively farmed this area where the the soil is so much more fertile than the sandy soil of the area that was later to become the New Forest. Within a three mile stretch of the Dean Valley three Roman villas existed, at East Grimstead, at West Dean, and at Holbury, the last two across the county boundary in Hampshire. Another Roman building was found

Heywood Sumner

159

nearer the Roman road at Winterslow. All of these buildings were presumably associated with the Roman road from Old Sarum to Winchester which William Stukeley noted as being very conspicuous in 1723, as it remains today in Stock Bottom where the *agger* (embankment) is very pronounced.

The old part of the church at West Grimstead contains incorporated in its walls much thin tile laid both herringbone pattern and in flat courses. These tiles, which appear to be Roman, may have come from the Roman villas in the Dean Valley, most probably from East Grimstead.

Deer Hunting and Deer Parks

The subject of deer hunting in this district was briefly mentioned earlier in this chapter in connection with Clarendon Park and Eyre's Folly at the west end of Dean Hill. The woods to the south of Dean Hill at the north-eastern extremity of the New Forest were extensively hunted and in addition to the great park of Clarendon already described, a number of other deer parks existed in the area.

In 1253 a licence was granted to William de Valence to impark a deer park at Newton and a 1256 document refers to Newton Park as recently enclosed. The location of the park at Newton is not definitely known. In the 13th century Newton lay in Melchet Forest, which explains the need for a licence to impark, although de Valence was the king's half-brother. It is possible that Brickworth (224241), one mile north-west of Newton and a seat of the Eyre family, may have been the site of Newton Park. In 1773 Brickworth was shown by Andrews and Dury as a landscaped park of some 150 acres, extending north-west beside the A36 towards Pepperbox Hill. A public footpath which runs north-west from Whelpley Farm (232240) to Pepperbox Hill follows the east edge of Andrews and Dury's Brickworth Park.

Further south there were more deer parks at Downton and at Loosehanger Copse (213912) on the edge of the New Forest. That a deer park existed at Downton is established by a report dated 13 October 1283 'touching the persons who broke into the park of John, Bishop of Winchester, at Downton, hunted therein, and carried away deer'. At the beginning of the reign of Henry VI in 1422, Bishop Beaumont of Winchester was regarded as the richest man in England, but the Bishop's parks at Downton were disparked in 1592. There are no known early references to a deer park at Loosehanger, but it was 'Losehanger Park' in the 1684 Parish Registers, and 'Lushinger Park' on Andrews and Dury in 1773.

Of Newhouse Park (218214), situated one and a half miles north of Loosehanger, Markham in his *Hundred of Frustfield* (1844) noted that the Elizabethan house was said to have been built as a hunting lodge for Sir

Thomas Gorges of Longford Castle who bought Newhouse in 1619. Newhouse was then (in 1619) described as 'The mansion late erected in scyte of the pales of the Park', and in *Modern Wiltshire* (1829) Colt Hoare wrote of: 'Newhouse, otherwise Tychebourne Park – at what time and by whom it was first imparked, I have not ascertained'.

The south end of Loosehanger Copse is crossed by a single public footpath running north-west to south-east (from 209191), and Newhouse is passed by the minor road from Redlynch to Whiteparish past Tichborne Farm (220219).

West Dean

This village stands on the county boundary with Hampshire at the eastern extremity of Wiltshire. The county boundary passes through the former Red Lion inn which has prominently on its facade the words 'WILTSHIRE' to its left and 'HAMPSHIRE' to its right. It is said that the coroner was once conducting an inquest in this inn until it was pointed out that he was in fact in the wrong county, a situation which he promptly remedied by moving the proceedings to another room.

Hidden away in the woods at the north edge of West Dean, not far from the modern church, is the 14th century Evelyn Chapel – sometimes called the de Borbach Chantry – now a mortuary chapel surviving from the old church of St Mary containing a fine series of monuments to the Evelyn family and to the Pierreponts who were descended from them. One monument to John Evelyn and family, dated 1627, includes kneeling figures. Sir John Evelyn was related to John Evelyn (1620-1706), the celebrated diarist. In his diary entry for January 1698-99 John Evelyn mentioned 'Sir John Evelyn, of Wilts, my father's nephew'.

Sir John acquired the estate at West Dean in the early 17th century and built a considerable manor house with elaborate formal gardens with canals in the Dutch style, shown by Andrews and Dury on their 1773 map of Wiltshire immediately north-west of the church and adjoining Dean Brook. The house and gardens were destroyed in 1819 when Charles Baring Wall pulled down the house and turned its outbuildings into a farmstead. Two public footpaths cross the site which is now in part a wooded wilderness of uneven ground immediately north of the railway.

The Wilton author Edith Olivier (1872-1948) was very fond of the West Dean chantry and used to motor there from Wilton with the artist Rex Whistler (1905-1944) to admire the monuments. Another writer associated with West Dean is Lady Mary Wortley Montagu (1689-1762). This lady, as a daughter of Evelyn Pierrepont, First Duke of Kingston, was a descendant of the Evelyns. She became an eminent blue-stocking writer with the reputation of being the most brilliant female wit of her time. In 1712 she eloped from West Dean in order to marry Edward Wortley-Montagu. One of Lady Mary Wortley-Monagu's achievements was the introduction in 1718 of vaccination for small-pox from the east, her husband having been ambassador to Constantinople.

During the 1750s the great naturalist and writer Gilbert White (1720-1793) – author of *The Natural History of Selborne* – was for a time curate of West Dean and used regularly to ride the thirty miles from his home at Selborne in Hampshire to West Dean.

A possible castle mound survives at the north end of West Dean village, together with a barn which was formerly a tithe barn belonging to Mottisfont Abbey near Romsey. This barn was later utilised to shelter and feed wild deer, which were conserved to be hunted in this area.

The Clarendon Way west of Clarendon Palace, looking west (Salisbury spire on the right).

Suggested Walks in South-East Wiltshire

12A: Dean Hill and West Dean (8 miles: map 184). 26·5·99

A car may conveniently be left at the National Trust car park at The Pepperbox on Pepperbox Hill beside the A36 at the west end of Dean Hill. The ridge of Dean Hill may then be followed for 2.5 miles eastwards as far as a point (250258) south of West Dean which may be reached by walking north down the road and then branching right on to the footpath which runs east of the road down to the village. After looking around West Dean, take the footpath which runs west from the new church a little north of the railway, passes the site of the East Grimstead Roman villa (at 234274), and continues to East Grimstead church at the extreme south of the village. A diversion north into East Grimstead will add three quarters of a mile to this walk. From the church walk south across the railway and for a mile along the droveway which makes straight for Dean Hill across the arable land. At the road at the foot of the hill branch right, ascend the hill, and return along the ridge to the start point.

This walk may be reduced by 3 miles to about 5 miles by starting the circular walk from West Dean and eliminating the stretch both ways from the A36 along the ridge past The Pepperbox to above East Grimstead. An alternative starting point for this shorter 5-mile option is from East Grimstead church where cars may be parked in the droveway near the railway (at 225272) south of the church.

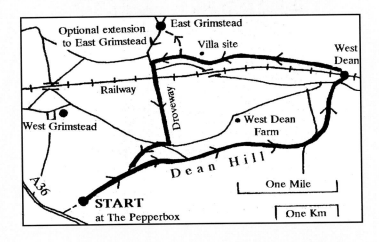

163

12B: Clarendon Park and Palace (6 miles or 3.5 miles: map 184).

Although access to Clarendon Park is rather restricted, a car may be left at Farley church and Clarendon approached by walking west by the footpath which crosses open land (through 215293). At 210294 east of Best's Farm turn north and at 210299 turn west and walk first west then north-west through Beechy Dean Copse. At 192304 turn south-west to reach the palace site at 182301. The site is private and should only be entered after obtaining the permission of the Clarendon Estate Office at Salisbury. The return may be east past Pitton Lodge, then south and east to follow the outward route back to Farley.

An alternative and shorter walk to Clarendon Palace of about 3.5 miles may be taken by walking 1 mile west from from Pitton Lodge, returning by the same route. This walk has recently (1997) been rather confused by the construction of several new stone-surfaced trackways through the woods.

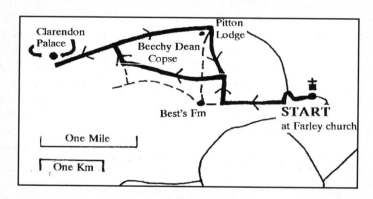

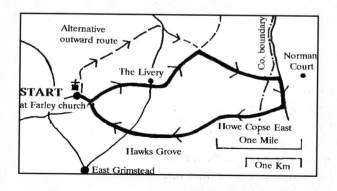

12C: Bentley Wood (6 miles: map 184) Map opposite below.
An alternative woodland walk from Farley church may be followed by walking east, first by road and then by footpath, past The Livery, then following the edge of Bentley Wood north-east to 247305. From this point follow the path south-east across Bentley Wood to the minor road west of Norman Court. Walk for half a mile south down this road (which is in Hampshire), then at 264293 turn west from the road, re-enter Wiltshire, and continue west across Howe Copse East. Pass Howe Farm and continue west (by path) and north-west (by road) back to Farley.

This walk may be extended by a mile to 7 miles by starting north from Farley church by footpath and continuing north-east through Hound Wood, by-passing The Livery and the north-west margin of Bentley Wood.

The Clarendon Way – a designated long distance footpath from Winchester to Salisbury – crosses the northern limits of south-east Wiltshire as defined for the purposes of this chapter. From Noad's Copse on the county boundary the way follows the line of the Roman road into Wiltshire, continuing through Middle Winterslow where the Roman road makes a slight realignment to run exactly west, crossing the River Bourne as a macadam road at Ford (163328) on its way to Old Sarum. At Middle Winterslow The Clarendon Way departs from the Roman road and diverges south-west through Winterslow to Pitton where, from near the school, it continues through Four Cottages (202312) and through the woods along the south side of Carverel Copse to pass immediately south of Clarendon Palace site. Its continuation to Salisbury is as a sunken way down King Manor Hill past Ranger's Lodge Farm and along Queen Manor Road, Milford Road and Milford Street to Salisbury.

The Clarendon Way is marked along its route by yellow waymark signs based on a Norman battle helmet. Leaflets on The Clarendon Way published by Hampshire County Council are sometimes available at Hampshire tourist centres, but not often in Wiltshire.

Correction to Walk 12B:
The suggested line from Clarendon Palace past Pitton Lodge is not a right-of-way. From Clarendon Palace ignore the map and follow the signed Clarendon Way to Pitton village and then south along road east of Pitton Lodge.

Conclusion

It is fitting that these two volumes devoted to *Exploring Historic Wiltshire* should end with a description of The Clarendon Way long-distance footpath, for this route has a particularly historic past. It probably originated as a prehistoric route following high ground to the north of the area that became the New Forest. Later it became a Roman road, and nowhere is the sense of history lurking in the landscape more strongly excited than when following the line of a Roman road across a now deserted landscape. The imagination can easily conjure up visions of first the Roman legions and later the civilian travellers going about their business during the subsequent *Pax Romana*, of Saxon war parties advancing along these roads during their take-over of Britain during the post-Roman Dark Ages, and of Viking war parties rampaging over England along these Roman roads which provided the most convenient way of travelling about the then heavily forested countryside. The way would have often been followed in Saxon times from the old Saxon capital of Winchester to Wilton Abbey at the south end of the Wylye Valley, and very name Clarendon Way commemorates the extensive use in medieval times of this road as a traffic route from Winchester to Old Sarum and to Clarendon Palace by the Court, and by the Norman Bishops of Winchester when visiting their Downton estates and deer parks during the early Middle Ages. It is the relationship that such historic events bear to the existing landscape which has provided the subjects for these two volumes on *Exploring Historic Wiltshire*.

Bibliography

The following is a short list of books for further reading. It is restricted to works that remain generally available although not necessarily in print. The publishers and dates given are those of first publication. Later editions are often available, sometimes by different publishers.

General Works (relevant to many chapters):
Wiltshire Archaeological and Natural History Magazine (very many volumes).
The Victoria County History of Wiltshire (several volumes).
J. Andrews and A. Dury: *Map of Wiltshire, 1773* (reduced facsimile, Wiltshire Record Society, 1952).
J. Aubrey: *The Topographical Collections of John Aubrey* (edited Canon Jackson, 1862).
W. Cobbett: *Rural Rides* (1826)
Sir R. Colt Hoare: *Ancient Wiltshire* (1812 and 1819).
R. Hippisley Cox: *The Green Roads of England* (Methuen, 1914).
Gover, Mawer and Stenton: *The Place-Names of Wiltshire* (Cambridge, 1939).
L.V. Grinsell: *The Archaeology of Wessex* (Methuen, 1958).
W.G. Hoskins: *The Making of the English Landscape* (Hodder & Stoughton, 1955).
I.D. Margary: *Roman Roads in Britain* (Baker, 1955).
H.J. Massingham: *English Downland* (Batsford, 1935).
H.W. Timperley and E. Brill: *Ancient Trackways of Wessex* (Dent, 1965).
G.N. Wright: *Roads and Trackways of Wessex* (Morland, 1988).

Chapter 7: Chute Causeway
H.J. Massingham: *English Downland* (Batsford, 1936).

Chapter 8: The Wylye Valley
G.B. Berry: *A Lost Roman Road* (Allen & Unwin, 1963).
W.H. Hudson: *A Shepherd's Life* (Chapter XIII) (Methuen, 1910).
E. Thomas: *The Icknield Way* (Chapter IV) (Constable, 1913).
E. Thomas: *In Pursuit of Spring* (Chapter IV) (Nelson, 1914).
R. Whitlock: *Salisbury Plain* (Hale, 1955).

Chapter 9: Wiltshire Selwood and White Sheet Downs

C. Cochrane: *The Lost Roads of Wessex* (David & Charles, 1969).

A. Major: *The Early Wars of Wessex* (1913).

E. Thomas: *The Icknield Way* (Chapter 1) (Constable, 1913).

Chapter 10: Great Ridge and Grovely Woods

W.H. Hudson: *A Shepherd's Life* (Chapter XXII) (Methuen, 1910).

As there are few publications on this area readers may wish to refer to the *Victoria County History of Wiltshire* (Volume 4) and the *Wiltshire Archaeological Magazine* (Volume 48).

Chapter 11: The South Wiltshire Ridgeways

C. Beaton: *Ashcombe: the Story of a Fifteen Year Lease* (1949).

C. Cochrane: *The Lost Roads of Wessex* (David & Charles, 1969).

D. Hawkins: *Cranborne Chase* (Gollancz, 1980).

W.H. Hudson: *Afoot in England* (Hutchinson, 1909).

General Pitt-Rivers: *Excavations in Cranborne Chase* (1887-98, privately).

E.H. Lane Poole: *Damerham and Martin* (Compton Russell, 1976).

H. Sumner: *The Ancient Earthworks of Cranborne Chase* (1913).

K. Watts: *Droving in Wiltshire* (Wiltshire Life, 1990).

R. Whitlock: *Salisbury Plain* (Hale, 1955).

Chapter 12: South-East Wiltshire

The extreme south-east of Wiltshire is poorly documented, except for a series of booklets published in the 1980s and 1990s by Michael Parsons.

Downton and other parts of the Avon Valley south of Salisbury are covered by Volume XI of *The Victoria County History: Wiltshire.*

Many of the writings of Ralph Whitlock contain information on this, his native countryside, and Clarendon Park is extremely well covered in the Report of the Society of Antiquaries entitled *Clarendon Palace,* by T.B. James and A.M. Robinson (distributed by Thames and Hudson, 1988).

The Clarendon Way is described by Barry Shurlock in *The Test Way & The Clarendon Way* (Hampshire County Council 1986). A leaflet on the same subject is also published by Hampshire County Council.

Index – Illustrations referred to in bold

172

More books from Ex Libris Press:

EXPLORING HISTORIC WILTSHIRE Volume 1: North

This is the companion edition to Volume 2: South and deals with the following landscapes of north Wiltshire:

Ridgeway Country; The Central Marlborough Downs; Wansdyke; Grigson Country; Calstone, Oldbury and Roundway Down; The Vale of Pewsey.

Volumes 1 and 2 are presented in a uniform format and together represent the best of Wiltshire, in terms of history, landscape and walking enjoyment.

176 pages; Price £7.95

THE PROSPECT OF WILTSHIRE

Words by John Chandler; pictures by Jim Lowe; maps by Karen Pigott

Jim Lowe has been photographing Wiltshire for many years; it is from his picture library that well known local author John Chandler has selected the images which feature here and which he introduces and captions in his informative and engaging style. Karen Pigott's hand-drawn maps add much to The Prospect of Wiltshire, the first and only full-colour book dedicated to the beauties of this special county.

Featuring: The Cotswold Fringe; The Infant Thames; Marlborough Country; Pewsey Vale; The Clay Vale; The Cloth Towns; Salisbury Plain; Chalk Rivers; The South-West.

112 pages; full colour throughout; hardback; Price £14.95

WHERE WILTSHIRE MEETS SOMERSET

20 Best Walks around Bath, Bradford on Avon, Trowbridge, Westbury, Warminster and Frome

Roger Jones; illustrated by Edward Dowden; maps by Karen Pigott

First published in 1982 and thereafter reprinted three times, this is an entirely new edition of the first book published by Ex Libris Press.

128 pages; fully illustrated; Price £5.95

We have several new Wiltshire titles to be published in 1998; please ask the publisher for details.

In addition to the above, Ex Libris Press publishes a list of around 60 titles on the West Country, Country Life and the Channel Islands. Our books are obtainable through your local bookshop or direct from us, post free, on receipt of net price.

Please ask for our free, illustrated catalogue describing all available titles.

EX LIBRIS PRESS 1 The Shambles Bradford on Avon
Wiltshire BA15 1JS Tel/Fax 01225 863595